Simplicity
and Success

Creating the Life You Long For

BRUCE ELKIN

Designed by Mark Hand.

National Library of Canada Cataloguing in Publication

Elkin, Bruce, 1943-
        Simplicity and success : creating the life you long for /
Bruce Elkin.

Includes bibliographical references.
ISBN 1-4120-0296-6

        1. Self-help techniques.   I. Title.

BF637.E44 2003   158.1   C2003-902510-1

TRAFFORD

This book was published *on-demand* in cooperation with Trafford Publishing. On-demand publishing is a unique process and service of making a book available for retail sale to the public taking advantage of on-demand manufacturing and Internet marketing. **On-demand publishing** includes promotions, retail sales, manufacturing, order fulfilment, accounting and collecting royalties on behalf of the author.

Suite 6E, 2333 Government St., Victoria, B.C. V8T 4P4, CANADA

Phone	250-383-6864	Toll-free	1-888-232-4444 (Canada & US)
Fax	250-383-6804	E-mail	sales@trafford.com
Web site	www.trafford.com	TRAFFORD PUBLISHING IS A DIVISION OF TRAFFORD HOLDINGS LTD.	
Trafford Catalogue #03-0665		www.trafford.com/robots/03-0665.html	

10   9   8   7   6   5   4   3   2

TABLE OF CONTENTS

Acknowledgments

Nearly twenty years ago, a book changed my life.

I'd been searching for a "path with heart" when Robert Fritz showed me how to create my own in *The Path of Least Resistance*. I studied and worked with Robert for nine years and have taught his principles and strategies for seventeen. His ideas and approach permeate this book. I have tried to make them my own and to amplify his amazing vision. Robert, I am grateful beyond words for your help and inspiration.

Special thanks to Bill Kittredge for teaching me how to write a good story and to Vicki Robin for help in the early stages of this project. I'm grateful, also, to all those great "simplicity" writers on whose shoulders I stand. I am equally grateful to all my wonderful clients and students, especially those whose stories I share here. You make it all worthwhile.

Thanks also to Doc Klein, Duncan Dow, Violet Van Hees, and Irene Whitney for almost daily support. Thanks to Elizabeth Lyon for teaching me how to write a proposal. Thanks to Rick Hill, Adina Hildebrandt, Sharon Wood, Lisa Cherry, and Andrea Rankin for reading and commenting on the manuscript. Thanks to Colin Rankin who sparked my confidence to take on this project so many years ago. Thanks to Tom Flemons for photos and fun. Thanks to Murray Reiss whose editorial help was invaluable. Thanks to Betty Hill for her insights into publishing and the book selling process. Thanks to Mark Hand for his simple, elegant cover design and text layout. Thank you *everyone* who helped with the project in any way. I appreciate it all.

Simplicity and Success is dedicated to my mother, Kay Elkin, without whom none of this would have come about. Finally, I wrote this book for Maia and Kai and for their children's children. May we leave them a world that they can love as much as I love mine.

Introduction

A Personal Odyssey

Downshifting. Cashing out. Living simply. Pundits such as Faith Popcorn tell us these trends are "hot." Fetzer Institute researcher Paul Ray estimates that twenty-four percent of US adults—forty million people, sixty percent of whom are women—are already "Cultural Creatives," strong advocates of self-creation, spirituality, ecology, and simpler lifestyles.

"The transformation," claims Ray, "is happening right in front of our eyes."

But wait! Haven't we heard such predictions before?

Yes. In the seventies, Harris polls claimed that most Americans wanted to consume less and preferred non-material pleasures. A 1976 Stanford Research Institute (SRI) report speculated there could be ninety million individuals practicing "voluntary simplicity" by the year 2000. "(A) major transformation," the authors suggested, could occur "in the coming decades."

However, instead of the predicted transformation, interest in simplicity quietly ebbed away. In its place, we got the eighties, a decade of unbridled greed, competitive consumption, and "looking out for #1." Although such oscillating behaviour confuses both pundits and simplicity seekers, it shouldn't surprise us. "Again and again," says David Shi in *The Simple Life,* "Americans have espoused the merits of simple living only to become enmeshed in its opposite."

Now, simplicity is hot again. It will get hotter as political and economic uncertainty grows. However, we'd do well to ask, *will it last?* This time, will we turn vision into reality?

A Personal Odyssey

I've been asking that question since the early eight*... ...*n I noticed myself oscillating between a desire for simplicity a*...* *...*ded high-school I started living simply in the mid-seventies. *...ce-based* environ-teacher, I lucked into a job developing a*...*

mental education program for a new outdoor center in the Rockies. Inspired by SRI's *Voluntary Simplicity (3)*[1] report and eager to participate in the coming transformation, I happily lived in teepees and camp trailers and made do with few possessions. I lived simply because it was the most direct way to live my new earth-friendly values and because environmental education didn't pay well. When I left the centre for a teaching job at a west coast university, I found it much harder to walk my talk.

Instead of teaching experiential education, cutbacks forced me to supervise student teachers in conventional classrooms. I hated it. I came home tired and frustrated. As joy and meaning in work went down, spending went up. Going to a restaurant or sending for pizza was easier than cooking. Buying a bottle of wine, a record, or a book would ease my bad feelings for a few days or hours. No longer forced to make do, do without, or do something else as I'd done on a low income, I purchased pleasures rather than created them. While I *espoused* the value of simple living, the trajectory of my life swung away from *acting* on that value.

Why, I wondered, *did I seem to have so little control over my own actions?*

After two years, I left the university, moved to a little island, and spent the winter writing. I traded handyman work for a small cabin and lived on $500 a month to show myself that I could live simply. I wasn't very handy and the job only lasted until spring. So I left the island and became an associate of the *Action Studies Institute*, a think tank that developed high-level action skills for individuals, business, education, and government. Over the years that followed, although I lived a simpler life than most of my contemporaries, I oscillated between my desire to live simply and my desire to craft a successful career. Sometimes my life was simple and uncluttered. Sometimes it was complicated and stressful. Oscillating between the two states confused me. So did the behaviour of th.. who abandoned the simple life in the eighties to join the orgy of upst. consumption that characterized that "decade of greed."

away, I nteract the despair I felt as I watched the simplicity trend ebb ature. ..nd re-read the classics of the simplicity and self-help literof a simple ired me. They motivated me. They validated my ideal the kind and wever, they didn't help me build momentum toward then slip back. f life I truly wanted. I'd try, make progress, and willpower, guilt, and positive thinking to *force* myself to practice what I preached but I felt as if I was swimming upstream. *Why*, I added to my list of questions, *could I not consistently walk my talk? How*, I wondered, *did people make real and lasting change?*

Throughout the late eighties and nineties, I devoted myself to exploring these questions. My Action Studies project involved researching the generic skills underlying practical creativity. *What skills and structure*, I wondered, *underlay the ability to create?*

Many experts described "creativity" as an inborn attribute, a gift from God to a special few. Others believed it was a breakthrough process to higher consciousness. Some associated it with mental illness. Others suggested that well-placed kicks or whacks to vulnerable body parts led to creativity. None of these explanations satisfied me. My understanding of generic skills convinced me there must be basic *skills* and *principles* that applied to any act of creation.

In 1985, when I discovered *The Path of Least Resistance* by Robert Fritz, the title put me off. However, the subtitle, *Principles for Creating What You Most Want to Create*, intrigued me.[2] I was delighted to find that Fritz's approach was *not* about taking the easy way out. Nor was it about "creative thinking" or "creative problem-solving." It was about the *act of creating*. Fritz showed how, by using a common form—an organizing framework and set of generic skills—creators consistently bring into being real and lasting results, in spite of the problems and circumstances they face.

Structure: The Key to Real and Lasting Simplicity

Just as water follows a path of least resistance laid down by the shape and structure of a stream bed, Fritz argues that our own energy and action follow a path laid down by the *structures* underlying our lives. In some structures, the path of least resistance leads to what we want; in others, it does not. In some, we advance toward desired results; in others, we oscillate.

Our life structures result from the way we arrange the relationships between our perceptions, ideas, values, beliefs, desires, fears, and external reality itself. If we're not aware of these relationships, it's easy to get stuck in structures that don't support our most important values and desires. *Either/or* structures, for example, give rise to oscillating patterns of behaviour. Moreover, there is a fundamental difference between the structure of problem-solving and the structure of creating — and between the kind and quality of results those structures produce.

Most problem-solving focuses on the *intensity* of a problem. Thus, it merely relieves the feelings associated with the problem. Taking aspirin provides relief from the pain of a stress headache but does nothing to change the behaviour that caused the stress or the structure that caused the stress-producing behaviour. Relief gives us the illusion that the problem is "solved." It allows us to keep doing what caused the stress and the pain. When the aspirin wears off, the pain returns. We're back where we started or worse, well on our way to ulcers.

So, "why not just solve the stress?" Again, because this kind of problem-solving focuses on the intensity of the problem, the same pattern unfolds. If we relieve the stress but don't change the structure that gives rise to it, we keep doing what caused it in the first place. Research shows that stress management programs can turn chronic burnout into acute breakdown by teaching people to cope with ever-increasing amounts of stress until they break.

By shifting our focus from solving problems to creating desired results, Fritz shows how to set up structures that guide energy and action toward what we most want. Instead of taking aspirin or solving stress, we can create structures that lead to stress free lives and work.

From Problem-Solving to *Creating*

Grasping the impact of structure on my behaviour changed everything. Recognizing the difference between problem-solving and creating made a huge difference in my approach to simple living and self-creation. I saw that a rich and simple life was not a solution to a problem, but rather a creation to bring into being. Over the next nine years, I studied and worked with Robert Fritz. I taught his approach to thousands of participants and hundreds of organizations. Using the principles of creating, I found it easier to *transcend* the either/or, problem-driven strategies that underlie so many quick-fix self-help and simple living approaches.[3] Using his approach, I wondered, *"Could I integrate simplicity and success? Could I create a simple yet rich, engaging, and successful life— and sustain it?"*

As the eighties gave way to the nineties, interest in simple living grew. Paul Ray's "Cultural Creatives" report claimed that many of us were already advocates of self-creation and simpler lifestyles. I hoped he was right. Still, I remembered the enthusiastic but faulty predictions of earlier pollsters. Could the growing interest in simple living be sustained? Or would it again ebb away on a changing tide of public interest?

Embracing Complexity; Creating What Matters

As my understanding of structure grew, I realized why I'd oscillated. I valued a simple, healthy, and sustainable life. I also valued "a good life" complete with challenging work, financial security, comfort, convenience, and respect. Unconsciously, I'd arranged my values into a dichotomy of desires, an "either/or" structure in which I pitted a simple, sustainable life *against* a rich, engaging, and successful one. In this *simplicity* v s. *success* framework, my values competed. Satisfying one increased the pull of the other. Attending to that value increased the pull of the first. Back and forth I swung, caught in an oscillating pattern generated by the unseen structure. As I focussed on getting rid of the frustration associated with that oscillation and fought against the complexity it generated, I lost sight of the results I most wanted to create.

Eventually, I realized that there were two kinds of simplicity: voluntary (freely chosen) and involuntary simplicity (poverty). I also realized that there were two types of complexity. Driven by unwanted problems, *involuntary complexity* leads to distracted effort and stress. Merely getting rid of (or relief from) what we don't like and don't want — clearing out clutter, for example — wastes precious life energy. Too often, it results in the reactive, temporary simplicity on *this* side of complexity. Clearing the clutter out of our lives and homes brings us relief, but, by itself, it does not bring the results we long for. Life is simpler and more successful if we freely embrace and transcend complexity by *creating* what matters.

Voluntary complexity is freely chosen and focussed. A potter throwing a thin-sided pot, a writer crafting a poem, or an entrepreneur growing a socially responsible business all experience complexity. However, because they embrace that complexity, it brings a focussed simplicity to their tasks and to their lives. Similarly, simplicity seekers who embrace life's complexity as the raw material of creating can create the deep, lasting, and satisfying simplicity on the *other* side of complexity. If clutter-clearing is driven by a vision of a well designed space such as a meditation corner — because you'd *love* to have such a space in your life — the space you create will be clutter free and stay that way.

Although creating a meditation space is more complex than clearing out clutter, that complexity is also more engaging. A clear, compelling vision of a space you'd love to create not only motivates you, it helps build the momentum you need to follow through to completion. Out of the gap between vision and reality, a useful, *creative* tension emerges. Creative tension is the engine of the creative process. You can use it to take actions that support your result. By focussing on a vision of what you want while embracing reality as it is, you set up a framework that contains and guides the resolution of creative tension. You also avoid the stress that comes with fighting against what you *don't* want. By working with the path of least resistance that forms between vision and reality, your actions naturally and easily flow toward what you want.

Creating Makes the Complicated Simple

As I shifted my focus to *creating what matters*, something remarkable happened. Not only was I able to create what I wanted, but my problems began to fade away. Carl Jung explained this phenomena when he said, "All the greatest and important problems of life are fundamentally insoluble.... They can never be solved, but only outgrown." Real change, he saw, resulted from a shift to a new level of consciousness. When patients embraced a more powerful interest, he explained, "the insoluble problem lost its urgency. It was not solved logically in its own terms but faded when confronted with a new and stronger life urge."[4]

By adopting a creating stance — by simultaneously focussing on what matters and embracing reality — simplicity seekers shift to a new level of consciousness and tap into one of life's most persistent urges: the urge to create. Creating, said jazz great Charlie Mingus, makes the complicated simple. The creative process, freely chosen, is simpler yet more powerful than problem-solving. The structure — the framework — of creating includes and transcends problem-solving. Thus, creating is a more reliable and effective structure in which to create results that matter. The enduring results on which civilization rests (art, music, literature, science, etc...) were not *solutions* to problems. They were *creations* that someone loved enough to bring into being. "All the great things," said Robert Frost, "are done for their own sake."

A Timely Offering

Simplicity to Success comes at a critical time. Many of us hunger for a way to transcend the complexity that comes from coping with jobs, careers, children, ambitions, fears about retirement, and the desire to leave a lasting legacy. Tired of seesawing between competing values, we are ready for a new approach, one that integrates values into an easy-to-manage whole. This book speaks to those who want to integrate personal freedom with intimate relationships, career achievement with healthy families, and personal fulfillment with work that provides meaning, challenge, and grace. It also speaks to those seeking to integrate spirit and soul into their everyday lives and work. Many of us are intuitively moving in this direction. For example, while browsing my local bookstore, I was surprised to find books on money displayed beside bestsellers on simplifying life and enriching the spirit. "What kinds of people," I asked my bookseller, "buy these different books?"

"The same people," she said, smiling sweetly.

I must have looked perplexed because she touched me gently on the arm and said, "There's a convergence of interests, dear, a kind of shared vision emerging."

It's my hope that *Simplicity to Success* will help you realize your part in this shared vision. I hope it will reinvigorate the simplicity movement, and elevate simplicity-seeking to a new level of mainstream interest. It provides critical next steps for the millions who have downshifted and millions more who contemplate doing so. It provides "simple-livers," downshifters, *and* "the rest of us" with a way to align vision, values, and actions so we more naturally and organically walk our talk. It will show you how to create results that honour who you are even as you strive to become the person you imagine yourself to be. *And to enjoy the process.*

The road to lasting simplicity and authentic success leads through new territory. To travel that road successfully requires new skills. We must master the higher-order skills to learn from our experience and to better apply the skills we already have. We need to:

- Understand the structure and dynamics of the creative process.
- Master the generic skills and practices common to all creators.
- Develop a life-long practice, a discipline if you will, of daily creating.

Together, these skills can empower and enable us to create—and sustain—the lives we most want. This book is about mastering these skills, integrating simplicity and success, and creating what matters most.

In Chapter 1, we'll examine the differences between solving problems and creating desired results. We'll see how one couple learned to transcend "dichotomies of desire" in favour of an integrated approach to creating what matters.

In Chapter 2, we'll examine overly-simplistic approaches to life-creation that produce the partial, temporary, and relief-driven simplicity that is found on this side of complexity.

In Chapter 3, we'll explore the deeper, more authentic and long lasting form of simplicity that is found on the other side of complexity. We'll see how creators embrace and transcend life's messy complexity and use it's energy to produce results that matter.

In Chapter 4, we'll explore the question "Simple Enough for What?" and see how two long-time simple-livers embraced complexity and created deep and lasting simplicity.

In Chapter 5, we'll explore the reasons why problem-solving is not a solid foundation on which to build a simple, yet rich and successful life. We'll examine six flaws in the problem-solving approach that make it a shaky foundation on which to create a life.

In Chapter 6, we'll shift our focus from solving problems to creating results that matter. We will examine the differences between *creativity* and *creating* and see that there is much more to creating what matters than just creativity or merely being creative.

In Chapter 7, we will explore the form of the creative process. We'll examine the basic structure — the framework — within which creators bring into being the creations they most care about. I'll outline the ten basic skills for creating almost anything and show you how they fit into the overall framework of the creative framework. I'll also show you how the core components of creating—vision, current reality, and action—interact with each other to make up the organizing framework—the container for creating—that is the creative process.

In Chapter 8, we'll explore Vision. I'll give you guidelines for getting clear about what matters, specifying the results you want to create, and crafting clear, compelling visions for those results.

In Chapter 9, I'll show how to assess current reality objectively and accurately. I'll explain why (and how) by holding Vision and Current Reality in mind at the same time, you can set up and tap the gentle but consistent power of creative tension.

In Chapter 10, I'll show how to use the dynamic tension inherent in the creative framework to orchestrate results through choices you make and actions you take. You'll see how creative tension works as the engine of creating and sets up a container for creativity.

In Chapter 11, we'll examine choice in the creative process. We'll see how creators set up hierarchies of choices in which smaller, less important choices support larger, more important choices. We'll see how commitment leads to action and to results no one could have imagined.

In Chapter 12, we'll look at Action Steps and the art and craft of everyday creating. We'll see how practice and planning interact. We'll see how creating is a learning process and how creators invent the processes that move them from where they are to where they want to be.

In Chapter 13, we'll see how to build momentum and follow through to final results.

In Chapter 14, we'll conclude with a word on commitment and completion.

Chapter One

Solving Problems?
Or Creating What Matters?

Find something you care about and live a life that shows it.
Kate Wolf

The telephone on my home office desk rang early one Monday morning.

"Good morning," I answered, "may I help you?"

"I hope so," said a worried sounding woman. "My name is Celia Carson.[5] My husband, Alverjo, and I have tried — several times — to simplify our lives, but can't seem to keep them simple. A friend told us you help people make changes that last, in spite of circumstances or adversity. Is that right?"

"It is," I said.

"Well," she said, sounding more enthusiastic, "we'd like to hear about your approach."

I get calls such as Celia's nearly every day. They come from those no longer willing to chase success at any cost but who can't define the success they want. They come from people who know what they want but don't know how to bring it into being. They come from concerned professionals, couples wanting to improve relationships, business owners eager to go beyond fads, boomers nearing retirement, and college students overwhelmed by an array of choices. Most want to simplify their lives *and* achieve success. But simplifying, they say, gets in the way of success. And striving for success leads them away from simplicity into complex, fast paced, and difficult to manage lives. Almost all say they feel stuck and stressed.

"I'm confused," says one. "How do we slow down?" "How do we get rid of clutter?" Many seem to be on the edge of desperation, frazzled by the fast pace of their complicated and frenetic lives. I often hear panic in their voices. "We're overwhelmed with problems!" Celia confessed. "It all seems so complex. Can you help us get rid of this mess?"

When I suggested that "getting rid of" problems was probably the main obstacle preventing her and Alverjo from creating what they wanted, an awkward silence came from Celia's end of the line. Some folks thank me politely at this point, then hang up. Those who stay on the line are skeptical. "You want us to think about what we want *before* we solve our problems? How will that help?" Celia, too, was skeptical, but agreed to do a short exercise to see the difference between *problem-solving* and *creating* as ways to produce desired results.

Solving Problems or Creating Results?

Experience the difference yourself by trying the following exercise. It only takes a minute.

First, think of the worst problem you currently face. By *problem* I mean something in your personal or interpersonal life that you do not like, do not want, and might even be desperate to get rid of. I do *not* mean challenges that engage and excite you.

Take a deep breath. As you exhale, close your eyes and focus on your problem. See it in all its detail. Imagine what will happen if you don't or can't solve it. Give your entire attention to this problem for a few moments. Then note how you feel.

Now, take another deep breath and shift your focus to something that you'd love to create — *something you'd love to bring into being* — but have not yet done so. Don't worry whether it is possible or not. Don't worry whether you have what it takes to bring it into being. For now, imagine that it *is* possible and that you have *already* created it. Imagine your result — your creation — as if it is part of your life. Focus on it in detail. Then note how you feel.

How did you feel when you focussed on your problem?

How did you feel when you focussed on the result you truly wanted to create?

Almost all participants report that when they focus on problems they feel "depressed," "dispirited," "down," "overwhelmed," "frustrated," "hopeless," and so on. Even those who prize their technical problem-solving skills report feeling this way when they focus on difficult personal and interpersonal problems. However, when they shift their focus to results they want to create, all of them report feeling "hopeful," "energized," "excited," and "ready to get at it."

In which stance would you prefer to spend your days — *and your life?*

While most people *say* they would love to spend their life creating, they confess they spend most of their time reacting or responding to problems. Not yet aware of the power of the creative process or how to invoke it, they depend on problem-solving to produce results. But problem-solving, as you'll see, is a shaky foundation on which to create what matters. Crafting a simple *and* successful life is not just about getting rid of what you *don't* like and *don't* want. It's about creating — and sustaining — what you truly *do* want.

A Frustrating Experiment in Simple Living

Celia and Alverjo came to my office for their first coaching session with worried frowns etched into their foreheads. Celia was a petite, bright-eyed, auburn-haired woman in her late thirties and seemed eager to learn. Alverjo, with dark, penetrating eyes framed by carefully styled, jet-black hair was several years older and seemed more reticent. They told me that during college they had been committed to social and environmental causes. "But once we graduated, we morphed into fast-tracking yuppies," said Celia. "We got caught up in the game."

"Pursuing success consumed us," admitted Alverjo. "Solving problems, achieving, and winning became our life. We enjoyed the challenge. We made big bucks. We bought a waterfront condo, a BMW, the whole bit."

"But it wasn't us," Celia added. "We couldn't keep it up."

After twelve frenetic, materially successful years, they burned out. Depressed, on the edge of breakdown and break-up, they cashed in their retirement funds and moved to the country. "We had to escape," Celia said. "The stress and competition of city life were tearing us apart."

"We cleared out all our clutter," said Alverjo. "We sold our Jeep and the Beemer. We sold our condo, our ski cabin, our leather furniture, and bought a used VW van. We moved to a rented cottage on a small lake with not much more than we could pack into the camper. We planted a garden, bought chickens, and settled in to enjoy the simple life."

"It was okay for a year," said Celia, "because it was new and novel. We read, went for walks in the woods, even joined a square dance club! But by the second year, we felt isolated and bored. The locals didn't really accept us. And, I know this sounds awful, but nothing exciting happened out there." She paused. "I mean, you can only talk about crops or quilting for so long. I tried to paint, Al took up carving, but our hearts weren't into it. We grew too dependent on each other's company. We gave it another year, then headed home."

Celia and Al returned to the city frustrated by their short-lived simplicity experiment. Although they still aspired to live simply, they were also hungry for a taste of the challenge and success they'd had. Almost immediately, though, they faced another *problem*. "We didn't want to plunge back into the life we'd left," said Alverjo, "but neither were we prepared to live without some of the comforts and conveniences we'd given up."

"We thought the solution was to find a middle way," said Celia, "a balance between challenging, good-paying work and a simpler, more spiritual, and environmental way of living." She glanced at Al, then continued. "But we can't find the balance point. We told ourselves 'Go slow, be careful, live simply,' but within months we got caught up in the old craziness again."

"We tried part-time contracts," added Alverjo, "but we either got too much work and tons of stress, or no work and couldn't pay our bills. We felt trapped. We still do!"

A Dichotomy of Desires

This dilemma is not unique to Celia and Alverjo. Many clients experience it. It arises when we arrange values into *either/or* structures. Setting up dichotomies of desire such as *success* **or** *simplicity* creates a dilemma that can seem impossible to overcome. We come by such dilemmas honestly. We are raised in a culture that values material comfort, competitive achievement, and the status, rewards, and respect that come with mainstream success. However, we are also taught to share, cooperate, and value the higher things in life. So, even as we strive for status, comfort, and material well being, most of us also yearn for a simpler, more fulfilling, and harmonious way of life. Because we are taught that the key to a successful life is balance, we assign these different desires equal value. But trying to balance values can be self-defeating.

One definition of "balance" is "to counteract; to neutralize the weight or importance." In trying to balance values we arrange them in a seesaw-like structure. Each value counteracts the other. Seesaws are inherently unstable. Even if we achieve balance, it's hard to sustain. A seesaw can quickly shift to an unbalanced "either/or" state in which one value predominates over the other. Just as quickly, it can shift the other way and the other value becomes most important.

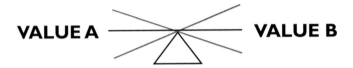

VALUE A   **VALUE B**

Such shifts seem to be out of our control. Unaware of this seesaw structure, Celia and Al shifted back and forth between their desire to simplify and their desire to succeed. They felt "trapped" in what seemed like a tug of war between competing desires. Seeking stability but unable to "find a balance point," they felt forced to trade off one desire for the other.

"We didn't want to look poor or have people feel sorry for us," said Alverjo, "so we let ourselves get overextended at work. Our lives got crazy and complicated again. To make ourselves feel better, we started buying stuff we didn't need. He chuckled to himself, then added. "When we slow down again, we'll probably see it as clutter and want to get rid of it all."

I pointed out that their approach focussed primarily on getting rid of what they *didn't* want. "That's not all we do," Al said, "but it's the most important part. By getting rid of what we don't want, we make a space for what we do want. That's the point of simplifying, isn't it?"

One reason for simplifying is to make a space in which to create what matters. But creating what you want takes considerably more thought, skill, and effort than merely solving problems or clearing away clutter. When you focus on what you don't want, you often jettison more than you intend to toss out. You end up longing not just for lost luxuries and conveniences, but also for the excitement, challenge, and rewards of achievement. You can learn to live without luxuries, but it's difficult and self-defeating to live without focussing on what truly excites you.

The alternative is to clarify and articulate what you *do* want and then use the creative process to bring it into being. When you are clear about and committed to what you most want to create, it's easier to see what is essential. It's easier to see what supports what matters and what does not. Your energy and actions flow more naturally toward what you most want to create. You may let go of clutter but you won't waste energy trying to "get rid of it." When faced with the stronger life focus that comes from creating, life's problems and clutter naturally fade away.

Success and simplicity are both important values. For most of us, it's not a case of achieving one or the other, or merely being satisfied with a bit of both. True simplicity and true success come from focussing on what you care about and living a life that shows it. "However," I explained to Alverjo, "when you're focussed primarily on problems and what you don't want, it's almost impossible to focus on simplicity and success in an integrated way. It can feel like your life is being driven by forces beyond your own control."

"Yes!" said Alverjo, snapping his fingers. "That's exactly how it feels."

Recognizing the Unseen Forces

We are influenced by many forces that we can't control. However, there are many that we can influence and ways to work with those we can't. The way, for example, that we arrange our values, aspirations, desires, beliefs, fears, and perceptions of reality sets up powerful *life structures* — organizing frameworks that guide our day-to-day behaviour.

As a streambed determines the flow of water along the path of least resistance, so too do the structures that underlie our choices and actions guide our energy along similar paths. Some paths lead to real and lasting results, others do not. Robert Fritz, author of the best-selling *Path of Least Resistance* books, has shown that only by changing the underlying structures that guide our surface actions can we generate behaviour that consistently leads to the real and lasting results we desire. The key to creating successful results is setting up life structures that work *with* the forces we encounter and lead us along a path of least resistance toward what matters most. When we can do that easily and naturally, we feel as if we truly own our own lives.

Transcending Dichotomies

A seesaw structure is an example of a *complicated*, difficult-to-manage life structure. Energy and action put into this kind of structure flow first in one direction, then reverse direction and flow the other way. Instead of trying to balance values and get rid of what you don't want, you'd do better to *integrate* values.

According to the Oxford English Dictionary, "integrate" means to "combine (parts) into a whole." Integrating values is a higher order form of simplifying than clearing out clutter. "Simple" means "easily understood or done; not compound; consisting of only one element or operation." Simplifying your life is not about getting rid of unwanted pieces or parts; it's about integrating those parts into one, easy-to-manage whole. To integrate values, you first need to clarify the relative importance of each value. Then you need to arrange them in a hierarchy of value in which the most important values are supported by less important values.

VALUE A Primary Value

VALUE B Secondary Value

This hierarchical arrangement sets up a simpler, easier-to-manage, yet more effective structure than a seesaw arrangement. In it, "secondary" values support "primary" values. Imagine that you, like Celia and Al, are struggling with a simplicity *vs.* success dichotomy. You have two choices: you can make *simplicity* primary or you can make *success* primary. If you choose success as your primary value, you will organize your efforts to simplify in ways that support both simplicity and the success you seek.

SUCCESS

Organize simplifying so that
it supports success

If you choose simplicity as most important, you will organize your efforts to succeed in ways that support your more highly valued goal of simplicity.

SIMPLICITY

Organize success so that
it supports simplifying

Either way, your life will be simpler, more successful, more consistently focussed, and easier to manage. The simplicity you create, especially if *simplicity* is your primary value, is more likely to be the real and lasting simplicity that is found on the other side of complexity.

Getting Rid of What You *Don't* Want Does Not Lead To What You *Do* Want

Unaware of the dynamics that give rise to behaviour, many clients make things more complex by defining dichotomies of desire as "problems" that they try to "solve" by getting rid of one of the conflicting values. Celia and Al called this approach "reprogramming ourselves."

"We took a workshop," said Celia, "in which they taught us to delete negative values."

"Did that work?" I asked.

"No," she said, laughing, "the conflict always came back. It was *so* frustrating!"

Deleting values doesn't work. Our minds are not machines. We want what we want, even if our values conflict. We contain contradictions;

that's part of being human. The way to deal with contradictions is to accept and transcend them. Forcing ourselves to deny or get rid of values leads to frustration, which becomes a new "problem." Getting relief from it is seen as "the solution." Over time, problem-solving draws us further away from our deeper desires. Our lives spin out of control. Our efforts become distracted. Complexity threatens to overwhelm us.

"We thought getting rid of stress and clutter by moving to the country would solve everything," said Alverjo. "But once the relief wore off, all that simplicity left a big hole. Back in the city, we're pulled in different directions. We want to slow down and simplify. But, like I said, other forces suck us toward career and consumerism. It gets confusing."

"Over the last two years," Celia added, "we've gone back and forth between one pole and the other. It's frustrating. Finding a simplicity that works is not as simple as the books suggest."

Simple Living: Lasting Trend or Shifting Tide?

I assured Celia and Al that it was not just individuals who oscillated between simplicity and success. The simple living movement itself has a history of oscillations. Twenty-five years ago, the buzz about the simple life was nearly as loud as it is today. But instead of the predicted "transformation," we got the eighties.

During that *Decade of Greed*, we shopped 'till we dropped, swapped compact cars for gas guzzling Sport Utes, and gulped down designer water, watches, and wearables with a vengeance. In spite of what we told pollsters, most of us did the opposite. I watched sadly as friends traded jeans and chinos for pinstriped suits, and VW vans for Volvo station wagons. I listened as conversations shifted from excited brainstorming around social, political, and environmental issues to serious, long-faced discussions about careers, stock trends, and opportunities in the financial and high tech markets. As the simplicity trend ebbed away on a turning tide of public interest, it left behind what Harvard sociologist Juliet Schor calls "the new consumerism."[6]

In *The Overspent American*, Schor says that since the eighties, consumers are no longer content to keep up with neighbours. They feel compelled to live the upscale lifestyles they see in glossy magazines and on TV programs like "Friends" and "Frasier." What were luxuries are now needs. Worse, in *Half Empty, Half Full*, Susan C. Vaughn says, "comparing ourselves with others who are better off and have things that we desire tends to make us feel envious and to create feelings of angry deprivation and frustration." This might explain why so many came out of the eighties feeling not only financially poor but poor in spirit.

Now, pollsters tell us that the tide has shifted again. "Along with self-creation and save the earth," says Faith Popcorn, "simple living is hot." However, we need to ask *Will it last?*

Muddling Toward Simplicity

"It's hard to live simply in the city," Celia lamented toward the end of our first session. "We're bombarded by ads for stuff we don't need. We *know* we don't need a DVD player or a big screen TV, but our friends have them, our colleagues have them, even our parents have them, so it feels like we're missing out on something. I don't know ... it's like we're somehow less successful than them, you know... if we don't have a new SUV. We've been trying to find a middle way, but Al and I can't even agree on what that would look like."

"Well," Al said "I'm all for simplicity, but not if it's boring, and not if I can't achieve the success and respect I think I deserve. Lately, I've been thinking it has to be one or the other. Go full-tilt, make money, and prove you can cut it while you can, then retire. Either that or just give up and go live in a tent. This back and forthing is too draining for me, too confusing."

"Oh, Al," said Celia, squeezing his knee.

It's *Not* All or Nothing

Before they left, I gave the couple an article describing the oscillations of individual simplicity seekers within the ebb and flow of the simplicity movement. I tried to assure Alverjo that the approach we would take would help him integrate the simplicity he wanted with his need to achieve the sense of purpose, engagement, and respect for which he so obviously longed. "It's not all or nothing," I assured them. "And we've already seen that it's more than balancing competing values." Success, I reiterated is about focussing on what you care about and living a life that shows it. It's about integrating values into a simple, unified, and powerful framework for making decisions, taking action, evaluating outcomes, making adjustments, and crafting results. It's about creating structures that embrace and transcend problems in favour of what matters.

To craft a rich and lasting simplicity, we do best to avoid approaches that pit us *against* problems and complexity. I'm not suggesting that we don't deal with problems. I am suggesting that we come at them from a different direction.

We'll look at how to do that — and at the different kinds of simplicity that *problem-solving* and *creating* produce — in the next three chapters.

Chapter Two

The Simplicity
On This Side of Complexity

I would not give a fig for the simplicity on this side of complexity, but I would give my life for the simplicity on the other side of complexity.

Oliver Wendell Holmes

"Do you really think people like us can create an enduring simplicity?" Celia asked during our next session. "I mean," she said, waving the article I'd given her and Alverjo, "you wrote about the possibility of trends petering out. Do you still have hope that we can create both simplicity and success — in spite of the problems and complexity we face?"

"I do," I said.

"Really?" she said, smiling.

"Really!" I said, smiling back at her.

To transcend problems and complexity, shift your focus from solving problems to creating what matters. When you get it right, your problems will shrink, even dissolve. With a *creating* focus, you're more relaxed, better able to flow. Your life is still complex, but it is a simpler, more engaging complexity. It's like the complexity that draws you into a beautiful painting or keeps you up all night reading a compelling novel. To shift your focus, it helps to understand that there are two kinds of complexity: one that is forced upon you and one you freely chose.

Involuntary complexity is driven by problems and circumstances. It leads to distracted effort. When you fight against it, seek relief from it, or try to get rid of it, this kind of complexity can confuse or even overwhelm you. Even if you succeed at simplifying, the best you achieve is the reactive, temporary form of simplicity that is found *on this side* of complexity.

Voluntary complexity, however, is freely chosen and focussed. A potter throwing a thin-sided pot, a writer crafting a poem, and an entrepreneur growing a socially responsible business also experience complexity. However, because it is freely chosen, engaging that complexity can bring a focussed simplicity to their tasks and to their lives. By embracing rather than fighting complexity, simplicity seekers are more likely to *create* the rich, deep and lasting simplicity on the other side of complexity. "The creative act," says Stephen Nachmanovitch, author of *Free Play,* "gathers an immense amount of complexity into a simple, satisfying notion."[7]

A Continuum of Simplicity Approaches

Simple living strategies can be arrayed along a continuum from temporary reaction to stress and financial difficulties all the way to the deep and lasting shift made by practitioners of "voluntary simplicity." The most popular strategy is "downshifting," the practice of voluntarily earning less money so you have less stress and more time and balance in your life. Some also downshift because they want to do something meaningful and to spend more time with their children. For many, however, downshifting is a problem-solving strategy that merely provides temporary relief from the stress and conflict of a consumption-driven life/work style. Indeed, just under half of downshifters surveyed by Juliet Schor said that they did so involuntarily, when they lost a job, were shifted to part time work, or had to take a pay cut.

Even the voluntary downshifters Schor studied said that when they downshifted, their desire for money and material things did not go away. It still acted as a force. It was still something that they wanted. When conditions change, as we'll see shortly, downshifters often experience a seesaw-like shift of dominance in which material values reassert themselves as a driving force.

Voluntary Simplicity

Although downshifting is growing in popularity, the most dramatic and enduring form of simplicity is "voluntary simplicity." Practitioners of voluntary simplicity reject the notion that becoming wealthy and accumulating piles of stuff is the best path to success. As Michael Phillips, author of *The Seven Laws of Money* puts it, "We offer our contribution to society by living in a way that shows others it is not necessary to 'make a lot of money' to live joyfully."[8] Those who practice voluntary simplicity have the material goods and services they need or have decided that they don't need most of them. Secure in home ownership and finances or focussed on a larger purpose — or both — they choose time over money, meaning over materialism.

True simple-livers go further than downshifters do. They transcend the trade-off between the desire for more money and a simpler yet higher quality, more integrated life. As we'll see in the next chapter, most of them use simplicity as a strategy for deliberately ordering their lives in support of an overarching life purpose that has meaning and passion for them. Simplicity, for them, is a way of focussing on what matters. Instead of shifting away from what they *don't* want, as most downshifters do, simple-livers wholeheartedly shift toward what they *do* want.

Two Ways To Be Rich

I met my first simple-liver in the early seventies. Ralph, a fifty-year-old family man, was a kind, rural, somewhat red-knecked, amateur philosopher who chose to live simply so he could, as he said, "have lots of time to just be and enjoy it." One day he told me, "A few years ago, I realized there were two ways to be rich: either have unlimited funds or don't need much money at all. I opted for the second way and have been happier ever since."

"I don't understand," I said. "How does *not* having money make you rich and happy?"

Ralph was an inveterate storyteller. "Well," he said, "some of my old college buddies had done well in business. They owned fancy horses and rode every weekend in the foothills. At least their wives and kids did." He punctuated this last remark by spitting tobacco juice onto the dusty ground, then continued. "I'd dreamed about riding since I was a kid. But when I saw what it cost my friends to buy horses, pay for stabling, feed, and lessons, and then outfit themselves and their families with all the tack, clothing, and other paraphernalia that goes along with being part of the horsy set, I realized I'd never be able to afford to do those things.

"However, a year or so after I started living simply on purpose, I helped a neighbour convert an old W.W.II supply warehouse into a riding arena. Naturally, we got to talking horses and I started whining about how I'd never be able to afford to own one. 'Hold on, Ralph!' my neighbour said. 'I know a purebred Appaloosa gelding you might be able to afford. He never spotted out so he can't be registered. The owner wants to sell him. Cheap!' My neighbour said that he knew the horse, knew its gentle temperament and its fancy bloodlines. 'It's a fantastic opportunity to own a great horse,' he said.

"But where would I keep him?" I asked.

"Keep him here," he said.

"But I can't afford stable fees or feed," I said.

"Keep helping me with the arena and he can stay free. I'll throw in lessons and an old bridle and saddle. Help me with the haying each fall and he can eat free all year."

"Well," said Ralph, smiling at me, then clearing his throat again, "I didn't have much money, but I was rich in time. I could afford to trade. So, I bought that Appaloosa gelding by paying half in cash and half in odd jobs. My friend put him up at his stable, and taught me to ride. Now I ramble in the foothills any time I want — without the pretentious horsy set stuff my friends put up with. That's a kind of happy that money can't buy."

I stared at Ralph as if I'd just seen the trick behind the magic.

He chuckled, picked up a hammer, then added, "My kids didn't think it fair that just I got to ride, so they made a deal with the neighbour to muck out the stalls if he'd let them exercise his horses. And you know son, there's no richer feeling in the world than riding along the top of those foothill ridges with your whole family and knowing it's hardly cost you a cent."

Amazed, I stood there shaking my head.

The Beauty and Dangers of Downshifting

Although I prefer voluntary simplicity to downshifting, I'm not suggesting that it is the only or best way to live a simpler life. I am suggesting that some simplifying strategies produce more satisfying and lasting results than others. The beauty of downshifting, for example, is that most of the boomer generation *can* afford to cut back their income in order to do things that matter to them. For some, simplifying a part of their life leads to simplifying all of it. In addition, it seems that when boomers take the lead, the rest of society follows.

However, the danger in downshifting lies in the fact that it is often a temporary compromise between the desire for more money and stuff (and what they symbolize) and the desire for a simpler life. Juliet Schor underscores this dichotomy. Although the downshifters she studied said they wanted a more meaningful life, most did *not* say they wanted a less materialistic life. "They would *prefer* more of both," says Schor, "but forced to choose, they make a lifestyle change that increases their time and reduces their earnings." Nearly half say that their shift is temporary.

Downshifters do live simpler lives and should be applauded. Many learn to transcend the time *vs.* money dichotomy as they experiment with simpler living. However, because the trade-off between time and earnings involves an *either/or* structure, they feel forced to chose between one value or the other. They risk falling into the same frustrating back and forth pattern that Celia and Al struggled so hard to overcome. If the trade-off between conflicting values and desires is not *fully* transcended, downshifters' behaviour will be inconsistent.

We want what we want, all of it, even if it contains contradictions and conflicting values. When values are not aligned in support of what matters, we're likely to oscillate between them and other important values. If downshifters feel "forced" to choose simplicity over stuff, there is always the danger that they will suddenly *upshift* when their circumstances change.

Upshifting

As a community organizer in the seventies, I experimented with cooperative simplicity. Although co-op members had a variety of reasons for living simply, I would never have guessed that any would suddenly drop simple living and become voracious upscale consumers. But, in the eighties, that's exactly what many did!

It was as if a pent-up demand for sacrificed comforts and conveniences exploded into an orgy of consumption. Later, I discovered that those who jumped on the consumption bandwagon had not valued simplicity for its own sake. Some were young and saw simple living as a cheap but temporary alternative to school or work. Others were activists who forced themselves to live simply as a way of fighting against things they didn't want, such as globalization and environmental degradation. Simplicity was just a tactic in their battle plan; it was not integral to their lives. When the spending spree erupted in the eighties, many from both groups dropped simplicity and flocked to the malls with most everyone else.

"I was tired of fighting," one of the ex-activists told me over lunch at his golf club, years later. "People weren't getting it. And I was tired of being poor. What was the point? Back then, I thought if you're not part of the solution, you're part of the problem. Well, I couldn't stop the juggernaut, so I thought I might as well get on board. Maybe I could change it from inside. Besides, I figured I deserved a reward for working so hard for so long."

When I asked him if he thought that he created change in his current position, he shrugged, took a sip of wine, then said, "I don't know. At least I have nice stuff to show for my efforts. And a good pension plan!" When I asked him if he was doing what he loved, his eyes glazed over. He turned away and stared out the window at the mountains on the far horizon.

Later, he told me he was depressed and thinking about simplifying again.

Involuntary downshifter, dedicated downshifter, or practitioner of voluntary simplicity — all are worthy experiments. However, if an approach is based primarily on reacting to problems and circumstances, it will almost always produce temporary, incomplete, and unsatisfying results. Unless the trade-off between values is *fully* transcended, the simplicity produced will almost always be the simplicity on *this* side of complexity.

The Simplicity on This Side of Complexity

To understand the simplicity on this side of complexity, it helps to distinguish between the terms *simple, simplistic,* and *oversimplification.*

"Simple," as we've seen, means "easily understood or done; not compound; consisting of only one element or operation." To *simplify* means to make things easier to understand or do, primarily by organizing them into some sort of meaningful unity. The power of creating comes from its structure, which integrates diverse pieces and parts into a unified, easy-to-manage whole. Most problem-solving approaches are either too *simplistic* or they *oversimplify* things.

The Concise Oxford Dictionary defines "simplistic" as "excessively or affectedly simple." Edward De Bono, author of *Simplicity*, says that *simplistic* means jumping from an observed phenomenon to a direct and simple explanation, missing out all the true complexity of the situation. When my activist friends adopted simplicity as a solution to complex problems, they took a *simplistic* approach.

People still simplistically claim "if you're not part of the solution, you're part of the problem." Simplicity approaches still focus followers on surface changes in behaviour based on problem-solving. The assumption seems to be that if you rid yourself of what you *don't* want, then what you *do* want will magically flow into the vacuum created by clearing out all that clutter. That's not simplicity; it's merely a *simplistic* reaction to unwanted circumstances.

It's as if I assume that my writing is blocked because my desk is cluttered and my notes are strewn about in piles. Thinking simplistically, I might assume that if I just tidy up my desk, file my notes in fancy multi-coloured folders, and arrange them in alphabetical order, then, magically, the words *should* flow. Nice theory, but it doesn't work in reality. Once my desk is clear and my notes tucked away in new folders, I still have to put words on paper. I have to shape the messy, confusing blur of ideas, fears, and desires that whirls about my mind into a coherent whole. I have to sort out what matters from what does not. I have to hone my skills and develop my craft. I have to make choices, take action, and bring into being what I *do* want. Assuming that clearing out the clutter will cause the words to flow is a simplistic, almost magical, way of thinking. It's not likely to lead to real or lasting results.

Taking Simplicity Too Far

De Bono distinguishes between *simplistic* approaches and *oversimplification*.[9]

"Simplistic," he suggests, "means that you do not understand the subject and so come up with a *simplistic* approach. *Oversimplification* means that you have simplified the matter too much and have left out important aspects of it. The oversimplification is not wrong, but it is inadequate because it is incomplete." Oversimplification is *simplicity* taken too far. When Celia and Al moved to the country, they over-simplified their lives. They ignored values crucial to their long-term fulfillment. Without that fulfillment, their lives became *too* simple to sustain.

"A thing should be as simple as possible," Albert Einstein advised, "but no simpler."

I've had clients who simplified so much that their lives became too austere to sustain. By adopting simplistic, unimaginative approaches, they threw fulfillment out with excess. Although they got great pleasure from reading, one couple cut books out of their budget. "Even used books are expensive," they explained, "and our local library is small." Another couple, who enjoyed a glass of wine before dinner, stopped drinking it. "It was self-indulgent," they said. A single man quit downhill skiing although he was good at it and got deep satisfaction from it. All of them lost something important by simplifying this way. Few of the changes they made lasted.

As well as introducing these kinds of clients to the skills and process described in this book, I do two things to help them recognize and get beyond their oversimplification. First, I tell them what Mohandas Gandhi told the Trappist monk Richard Gregg when he confessed that he had a greedy mind and wanted to keep his many books. "Don't give them up," said Gandhi. "As long as you derive inner help and comfort from anything, you should keep it. If you were to give it up in a mood of self-sacrifice or out of a stern sense of duty, you would continue to want it back, and that unsatisfied want would make trouble for you. Only give up a thing when you want some other condition so much that the thing no longer has any attraction for you, or when it seems to interfere with that which is more greatly desired."[10]

Simplicity is not about sacrifice. It's about focussing on what matters, on what you truly want to create. When you simplify in this focussed way, you do not have to give up things you care about. There is no "unsatisfied want" that would make trouble, no conflict between desire and duty that is left hanging. There is less chance of falling into an oscillating pattern. Of course, if you're not sure what you want, it becomes much harder to focus.

The other thing I do for clients who oversimplify is point them to the chapter on fulfillment in Joe Dominquez and Vicki Robin's book, *Your Money or Your Life?*[11] I suggest that before cutting back some aspect of their lives, they ask themselves these two questions:

> 1. *Do I receive fulfillment, satisfaction, and value from this item or activity in proportion to the life energy I have to spend to get it or do it?*
> 2. *Is this expenditure of life energy in alignment with my values and life purpose?*

If the answer to both is *yes*, I suggest they keep the item in their lives. If the answer to either or both is *no*, I suggest they try letting it go. When the couple who cut wine out of their budget examined their strategy through these lenses, they decided they had gone too far. They decided to put wine back into their daily routine by learning to make their own. Over time, they became excellent wine makers. Their dinner conversations — and their lives — were enhanced not only by the pleasure of sharing great wine but also by the pride and self-respect that came with successfully mastering the complexities of the wine maker's art.

The fellow who quit skiing realized that he had cut out a major source of satisfaction. When he decided to return to his sport, he did so without feeling obligated to buy into the consumption surrounding it. He volunteered as a "visitor's guide" at the ski hill and got to ski free each day. "That's how I met my wife," he told me, grinning like a man who'd just won the lottery.

When the couple who'd cut out books reconsidered their decision, they saw that they had sacrificed fulfillment to achieve frugality. When I asked why such strict frugality was so important, they realized they had used the same competitive approach to simplifying that they had used to generate professional success before simplifying. They saw they had simplistically tried to become "the most frugal simplifiers around." Realizing that such a rigid, policy-driven approach had given them great grief before simplifying, they relaxed their approach and reintroduced books into their lives. "That was a great lesson," one told me, "because it wasn't just about books. Unconsciously, I'd followed a simplistic, self-imposed policy that made a competition even out of simplifying. After I stopped feeling foolish, I was glad I discovered that tendency in myself. I now channel my competitive urges in more beneficial ways."

If, after thinking about Gandhi's advice and Dominquez and Robins' questions, clients still want to give something up, so be it. However, most find that simplicity becomes easier to create and sustain if they consider fulfillment as well as frugality as criteria for success.

Transformation Is Not Likely On *This* Side of Complexity

Living by self-imposed policies rather than a vision of what matters, giving up things from which you draw inner comfort, adopting simplistic, quick-fix, problem-solving approaches, and over-simplifying are all strategies that lead to the unfulfilling and difficult to sustain simplicity on *this* side of complexity. These partial strategies focus on pieces of your life rather than the whole. They are often driven by a desire for relief rather than results. They are reactive; they turn away from complexity. Therefore, they do not provide a stable foundation upon which to create what matters. The simplicity they produce neither satisfies, nor lasts. It will *not* lead to the transformation predicted by the pollsters — not in individuals and not in society as a whole.

Nonetheless, as I told Celia and Al, I *do* have hope that simplicity can be an essential element in the rich, well-lived lives of millions throughout this country and the world. There *are* hopeful signs in the latest wave of simplicity seeking. It is more mainstream and urban than the last wave. Paul Ray's *Cultural Creatives* are approaching the age when meaning takes precedence over materialism. Millions of copies of simplicity books have been sold. The trend has spawned simplicity circles, study groups, on-line forums, magazines, and microcosmic cultures of simplicity in cities like Seattle, Ann Arbor, Michigan, and Eugene, Oregon. The movement is diverse. A great deal of exploration and experimentation is taking place. There are as many different approaches to simplicity as there are seekers after it.

I am concerned, however, that many simplicity and self-help approaches rest on oscillating, problem-focussed foundations. Such platforms rarely generate results that last, especially in the face of adversity.

"The key to sustaining results in our own lives *and* in the simplicity movement," I suggested to Celia and Al, "is to develop approaches that move from the reactive simplicity on this side of complexity to the deeper, more engaging simplicity on the other side."

They were excited by the prospect, but still skeptical about what they called "having it all." I could see it was going to take both explanation and experience to convince them.

Chapter Three

The Simplicity
On the Other Side of Complexity

Simplicity before understanding is simplistic;
simplicity after understanding is simple.

Edward de Bono

"I'm not so sure," Alverjo said at our next session, "that I get the difference between the simplicity on this side and the simplicity on the other side. It still seems to me that the most effective thing to do is clear out clutter and make a space for creating."

"Did it work," I asked, "when you cleared out everything and moved to the country?"

"No," he said, "not really."

"Maybe," I suggested, "you had your priorities reversed?"

"What do you mean?"

"You say that you have to clear out clutter *before* you can simplify. But what if you simplified by focussing on what matters and then just let go of whatever doesn't support that focus? Clearing out clutter becomes secondary, just one of many steps you take towards creating a simple, focussed, and successful life."

"Hmmm," said Al. "It still seems a little backwards."

It can be difficult to take in new concepts. Faced with a challenging concept such as *the simplicity on the other side of complexity*, we hold on to what is familiar. Clinging too tightly to what we think is "the right way" can prevent us from grasping the new. It can seem as if it's an *either/or* decision. Some experts, for example, claim that you have to "unlearn" what you know before you can learn something new. I don't agree. Just as you don't have to unlearn English to learn Spanish, you don't have to get rid of old ideas, concepts, or skills to learn new ones.

With practice, anyone can learn and apply this *creating* approach. They may have to struggle a bit with the new concepts, work on new skills, and develop fluency in them before they can habitually choose the new approach over the old. But eventually, they can master it.

During our next few sessions, Celia and Al worked to relax their grip on their simplistic, problem-focussed approach. Gradually, they began to grasp the difference between the reactive simplicity on this side of complexity and the deeper, more engaging simplicity on the other side. "I can see," said Celia during one of those sessions, "that reacting to problems without being clear about what you want can lead to more problems. But, like Al, I still don't get why simplifying isn't about getting rid of complexity."

"Yeah," added Alverjo, "isn't it complexity that makes our lives so messy and miserable?"

"No," I said. "Complexity is an integral part of a simple, well-lived life. It's what we do with complexity that makes us miserable."

Messiness Can Be Beautiful

Complexity is not a problem. It is not something to avoid or eliminate. Complexity makes fine wine enjoyable. It keeps us up at night glued to the plot of a gripping novel. It keeps airplanes in the air. It makes conversation an art form. It keeps living systems healthy. Yes, it *is* often messy, but it doesn't have to be miserable. Life, leading-edge theorists tell us, thrives on messiness. "Let's face it," said Donella Meadows, a systems thinker and practitioner of deep simplicity, "the universe is messy. It is nonlinear, turbulent, and chaotic. It is dynamic. ... It self-organizes and evolves. It creates diversity not uniformity. That's what makes the world interesting, that's what makes it beautiful, and that's what makes it work."[12]

Messiness is an essential aspect of life. And of individual lives.

"Through messy, parallel activities, life organizes its effectiveness," says complexity expert Meg Wheatley in *A Simpler Way*[13]. "It looks like a mess. It is a mess. And from the mess, a system appears that works."

Wheatley is talking about "emergence," the idea that order arises out of chaos. That doesn't mean we should tolerate messes or let ourselves be overwhelmed by chaos. But nor should we push so hard to make things orderly that we fail to leave space for the magic of emergence to occur. To navigate complexity, we need to embrace *and* transcend life's messiness. Instead of trying to get rid of it, it's better to work with complexity and rise above it. Emergence is more likely to work for us if we're *creating* than if we're stuck in problem-solving.

Embracing and Transcending Messiness

Everyone's life can and does get complicated, even chaotic. That's why simplicity appeals to so many. However, you do not have to become upset at complexity or "solve" it. It's a mistake to try to "fix" messy systems. Trying to "solve" challenges that are not really problems can lead to far worse problems. Although lives, work, and relationships may *feel* messy, it doesn't help to think that they are broken; they're not. All normal lives include periods of chaos, especially during times of change. Accepting and embracing disorder as part of your creative process produces better and more lasting results than trying to fix or get rid of complexity.

However, because many people do not know how to deliberately create what they want, they still see complexity as a problem to solve. This might explain why the market for relief-based approaches such as problem-focussed self-help, therapy, and organizational consulting continues to grow — in spite of a large body of research that shows that most problem-focussed approaches do not work. At best, they provide temporary relief from intensity; at worst, they produce more and worse problems. Problem-solving is an attempt to control what happens in a system. Although it works in mechanical systems, a basic feature of messy, living systems is that, to a very large degree, you *can't* control them. You can, however, *influence* them.

Influencing messy systems is different than controlling mechanical ones. It's not a direct cause and effect process. It's more organic, more like growing results in a garden than producing them on an assembly line. It's like engaging in a dynamic conversation in which both parties emerge with new knowledge, greater understanding, and a deeper sense of intimacy. It requires a subtle approach. "We can't control systems, or figure them out," said Donella Meadows. "But we can dance with them!"

The word "control" comes from Middle English, meaning "to exercise restraint over." "Influence," on the other hand, is derived from the Latin word *fluere*, "to flow." To influence complexity — to produce results you want in spite of it — go with the flow. Work *with* the forces in play. Just as a sailor can't "exercise restraint over" the wind, tides, and currents, you can't control the many forces at play in your life and work. This does not mean that you're helpless in the face of those forces. As the old saying goes, "You can't direct the wind, but you can adjust your sails."

To influence complexity, don't try to force things to happen, or to get rid of them. And don't let them randomly push you around. Instead, dance with them. Determine where you want to go *and* where you are, then use the energy of the forces in play to set up a path of least resistance and steer a gentle course toward what you want to create. Seeking to control complexity is a simplistic strategy that will make your life more complicated and confused. Working with life's messiness by creating what matters is a complex strategy that embraces and then transcends complexity. It leads to the deep and lasting simplicity on the other side.

Focussed Simplicity in Daily Life

So what does the simplicity on the other side of complexity look like? It's easy to describe physical examples of the simplicity on the other side of complexity. It looks like expert tango dancers whirling easily and elegantly across a polished dance floor. Neither is in control of the other. Each plays a critical part in the passionate expression of music through movement. What emerges from their interaction looks simple and effortless. However, that simplicity results from a complex interplay of forces and counter-forces in which the dancers hover on the edge of chaos. If they get too complex, they court disaster. If their dance is not complex enough, it is stiff and stilted. The simple elegance that entrances onlookers results from the dancers' ability to move through complexity to the simplicity on the other side.

The simplicity on the other side of complexity looks like the graceful power of professional athletes. The great Formula One auto racing champion Sterling Moss said that winning was simple. "I have to give it my all. If I give 9/10ths, I lose; if I give 11/10ths, I die. Only if I give 10/10ths during a race do I win." That's a complex kind of simplicity.

The simplicity on the other side of complexity looks like the heart surgeon who in the chaos of life and death trauma maintains her steadiness of hand, her precision, her endurance, her powers of focus and concentration, and her grace. That grace is the simplicity on the other side of almost overwhelming complexity.

Finally, although it is harder to describe, the complexity on the other side of simplicity can be seen in any work of creation. Recall Stephen Nachmanovitch's assertion that creating "gathers an immense amount of complexity into a simple, satisfying notion." Through the creative process, creators work with a myriad of internal and external forces to produce the simple elegance of a completed creation. "Anyone can make the simple complicated," said jazz giant, Charlie Mingus. "Creativity is making the complicated simple."

Creating Makes the Complicated Simple

Instead of trying to *make* things happen in your life, work, and relationship, you'd do better to create spaces in which what you want can emerge out of the complexity of your life's flow. That's how creating works. As you'll see throughout this book, by keeping vision and reality in mind simultaneously and working with the tension that arises between them, creators set up a dynamic organizing framework that acts as a container for creativity.

Just as a magnetic field organizes iron filings, the creating framework aligns daily choices and actions in support of the results you choose to create. As a creator, working within a framework that is driven by vision, grounded in current reality, and focussed on results, you can remain open to the forces in play. You can embrace surprise and novelty. You can take what emerges from your creative process and shape it into what you want to create.

"The future can't be predicted," cautioned Donella Meadows, "but it can be envisioned and brought lovingly into being. Systems can't be controlled, but they can be designed and redesigned." If you think of your life as a complex, self-organizing system, you'll see that life design and life creation are far more powerful strategies than problem-solving.

Creating makes the complicated simple through *focus*. Focus cuts through clutter. It brings the disparate elements of life into alignment. As in laser light, focus generates coherence. It also generates energy, the power you need to make your dreams a reality. Moreover, by unifying all aspects of an undertaking in support of a deeply desired result, focus simplifies. It makes things easier to do and more enjoyable. What does-n't matter stops acting as a force; the unnecessary falls away. You're left with what matters, with the simplicity on the *other* side of complexity.

Working Through Complexity

Thirty years ago, I found myself in a complicated mess from which it seemed impossible to escape. As a young high school teacher, I loved kids, teaching, and learning but I hated the rigid policies and proce-dures of the system in which I taught. Feeling trapped in an untenable situation, I suffered a perambulating nervous breakdown. I stumbled through several years on the edge of deep depression and almost unbearable anxiety. I did not act with integrity. Marking time, doing what other people thought was best, I failed to express my highest val-ues and aspirations. During my last year of teaching, confusion so near-ly overwhelmed me that I relied on daily doses of Valium and before-dinner beers to keep the ferocious anxiety I called *The Terror* at bay.

I see now that my anxiety arose out of my inability to deal with a complex dichotomy of desires. I wanted to be a great teacher. I wanted to serve students by designing open, student-centered "environments for learning." I wanted to draw out the best in my kids, not merely serve what I thought was a mostly mindless system. Ironically, although I had higher performance standards for students, my authoritarian colleagues objected to my flexible methods. They insisted I "stick to the curricu-lum." But I saw that the curriculum bored kids as it had bored me in high school. It didn't challenge or engage them; it failed to draw out their best. Studying it depressed them as it depressed me to teach it. Every day, I thought about quitting.

I didn't, though, because I didn't know what to do instead. I'd done eight years of post secondary schooling in sociology, psychology, and education. I'd thought about becoming a journalist but couldn't imagine going back to school to train for another profession. Moreover, I had debts to pay. In spite of my high-thinking principles, I craved the secu-rity of my regular school board pay cheque. So, in a compromise that came close to killing me, I stayed on.

Teaching became a dismal, passionless chore. My depression deep-ened. I felt trapped, as if my life would always be that way. I lived in a constant state of near panic. In my most vulnerable moments, *The Terror* attacked like a sharp-clawed raptor, ripping at my confidence and self-esteem. At times, I thought it would never end; I thought about taking my own life.

Somehow, with the help of a sympathetic principal, a job teaching skiing at night, and my daily regimen of Diazepam and Dutch beer, I struggled through the year. During the last quarter, I heard about a new graduate program in Environmental Design that claimed to integrate environmental studies, architecture, and urban design. I applied and was accepted based on a proposal to "design and develop experiential environments for learning." I wasn't sure I knew what that was, but I looked forward to exploring it.

Being accepted into Design School brought relief from the worst of my anxiety. I still felt uptight, but *The Terror* stayed away most nights. My depression lifted. But once in the program, I found myself pulled in too many different directions. One professor suggested I focus on ecology. Another wanted me to do urban design. For a while, I considered designing ecologically friendly buildings. Then I thought, "What about all the environmental issues that need attention?" I careened from one interest to another like a pinball. My anxiety crept higher. *The Terror* began to haunt my nights. Sleep became a forgotten luxury. Late one sleepless night, trying to calm myself by reading about "The Land Ethic" in Aldo Leopold's *A Sand County Almanac*, I had a kind of epiphany. Leopold claimed that our challenge was not to build roads into lovely country, but to build receptivity into the still unlovely human mind.

I read and re-read the line a dozen times, letting it burn through the mess in my mind.

That was it! Suddenly, I knew what I wanted to do. Out of the mess of the past year and a half, a clear and powerful focus emerged. I wanted to build receptivity toward nature and the processes of life into young people's minds. I wanted to build receptivity in them toward their own power. I wanted to help them develop their capacity to create what truly mattered in their lives — in harmony with the natural systems on which all life depends. Instantly, my life became simpler and richer. Everything I wanted to do coalesced around my emerging purpose. Decisions, choices, and actions lined up in a coherent way. What didn't matter fell away like shells off newly hatched chicks. The confusing mess in my mind formed itself into a clear, focussed, and purposeful plan of action. What had been so complicated became elegantly simple.

Over the next few months, I drafted a design of a wilderness-based learning program to help young people develop character and mastery through challenging but environmentally sensitive outdoor experiences. Because the faculty refused to support my proposal, I left the university. I found sponsors in another school board and the YMCA. I spent the next year working part-time for the school board's *Action Studies Team*, learning how to develop character and creativity in kids, and developing my environmental education skills as a trainer for *The Institute for Earth Education*. The next summer, I piloted two three-week long sessions of *Earthways: Experiences in Personal and Environmental Exploration*. It was a huge success. During the three years I ran Earthways and follow-up programs during the winter, I learned a great deal about navigating complexity and integrating the bits and pieces of my life into a coherent whole.

From A Heap to A Whole

"A heap," said Ken Wilber in *A Theory of Everything*, "is not a whole."[14]

Just as a heap of bicycle parts does not give you a bike that you can ride, neither does a heap of disconnected reactions to problems and circumstances add up to a simple, yet rich, whole, and satisfying program — or life. Although I'd lived a simple life as a graduate student, the simplicity was external. My interior life was a grotesque example of complicated messiness caused by trying to solve too many problems and fight too many battles at one time. When I started Earthways, the pieces and parts of my life began to line up around my newfound purpose.

The shape of my life shifted from a heap to a whole. I took on the attributes of healthy, fully functioning systems. I became more creative, stable in my moods, and consistent in my actions. I became resilient, able to bounce back quickly from setbacks. I reached out to others for help, adding a diversity that hadn't previously been part of my life. Most of all, keeping my purpose in mind and steering towards my vision, I sustained the changes I made in my lifestyle. I lived simply because doing so made it easy for me to focus on Earthways and because the kids saw my lifestyle as a model to emulate. Besides, I enjoyed the simple, focussed elegance of that lifestyle.

Freedom *From*... or Freedom *To*...?

Many people think of freedom as the absence of restraints or restrictions or as relief from negative feelings associated with problems. However, there is more to freedom than mere relief or just being free *from* restraints. As with simplicity and complexity, there are two kinds of freedom: *"freedom from"* and *"freedom to."*

Freedom to is harder to define than *freedom from*. It involves the complex interaction of all the skills, knowledge, abilities, and tools that a person needs to actually *do* something. Without the ability to act — to create what matters, for example — freedom from restrictions means little.

In *To Have or To Be?* psychologist Erich Fromm described the kind of difficulties faced by young people such as my activist co-op colleagues from the sixties.[15] Such young people, he suggested, "had not progressed from *freedom from* to *freedom to:* they simply rebelled without attempting to find a goal toward which to move, except that of freedom from restrictions and dependence." Fromm called this approach "naïve narcissism" and said it worked only as long as the euphoria of rebellion lasted. Narcissism is a kind of "Don't tell me what to do" stance. "Many," Fromm said, "passed this period with severe disappointment, without having acquired well-founded convictions, without a center within themselves. They often ended up as disappointed, apathetic persons — or as unhappy fanatics of destruction." Many of them, I think, became upscale consumers in the eighties and nineties, afflicted with the soul- and culture-killing viruses "Affluenza" and "Boomeritis."

Fromm thought that those who focus on *freedom to* are "moving in the direction of being." He said that they represent a new force that will transcend the 'having' orientation of the majority. I agree. Focussing only on *freedom from* — reacting or responding to what we don't want — leads to involuntary complexity and to the simplicity on *this* side of complexity. Focussing on *freedom to* — on what matters and taking action to bring it into bringing — leads to voluntary complexity and to deeper, lasting simplicity that arises out of the creative process. Because many of those who focus on *freedom to* are also seeking that deeper, more lasting form of simplicity, they may well be on the leading edge of both personal and social transformation.

The Soul's High Adventure

Moving from a heap to a whole and from *freedom from* to *freedom to* is a matter of setting out what matters most and then setting yourself firmly on the path toward creating it. When I'd finished my Earthways story, Al said, "I think I get it. It's like that George Bernard Shaw quote about the true joy in life is to be used by a great purpose. When viewed in that context, complexity seems less threatening."

Simplicity and success are about focussing passion and purpose. Purpose and passion give power to our lives. Creating a rich, engaging, and rewarding simplicity does not have to be a problem to solve, seek relief from, or avoid. It can be a passionate challenge, a daring experiment, an example of what Joseph Campbell called "the soul's high adventure." The challenge of creating the real and lasting simplicity that is found on the other side of complexity is to embrace and transcend the circumstances of our lives and bring into being what we most want to create. If soul is, as some suggest, the unifying principle — the power and energy arising from the core of our being — then *creating* the simplicity on the other side of complexity is surely a soul-making adventure. In the next chapter, we'll see how purpose and passion can help us embrace complexity and create the deep, lasting simplicity we long for.

Chapter Four

Embracing Complexity; Creating Simplicity

One must feel chaos within to give birth to a dancing star.

Nietzsche

As Celia and Al grasped the difference between the two types of simplicity, they recognized examples in their own lives. In one of our coaching sessions, Celia described a familiar situation in which a mess transformed into simple, elegant order.

"We were in the middle of a bitter, messy argument," she said. "Al accused me of all kinds of things and I accused him of worse. Things got so heated and complex that we forgot why we'd started arguing. It was a real mess. I didn't think we'd ever get out of it. Then, out of nowhere, Al stopped arguing and just looked at me with compassion in his eyes. 'I'm sorry Cee,' he said. 'I love you. I don't want to fight anymore.' I was shocked, but in an instant, my defenses fell away. I felt very connected. It hit me that this experience of love and connection was so much more important than winning an argument. My love came surging back. I threw my arms around Al and kissed him. As he kissed me back, I knew we'd made it through the mess and were headed for the simplicity on the other side."

Celia clarified that this moment didn't magically solve all their problems. However, it did help them reconnect with what mattered. "As we focussed on what mattered," Celia said, "problems just kind of melted away. What was left were core issues that we had never really examined. Buoyed by our renewed feelings for each other, we focussed on those issues from a creative stance. By agreeing about what we really wanted in our relationship, we were able to accept that there could be differences in how we each created our part. We experimented with ways that let us both get what we wanted. And it worked."

Love as a Simplifying Force

"This whole adventure of creativity," says Stephen Nachmanovitch, "is about joy and love."

Love — "an intense feeling of deep affection or fondness for a person or a thing" — is a powerful force. It motivates. It focuses. It simplifies. You don't create with your intellect alone. Carl Jung said that the creative mind plays with the ideas and objects it loves. Creators love creations enough to do whatever they need to do to bring them into being — regardless of what they encounter along the way. Love is the force that drives the act of creating. Creators' love for creations keeps them focussed, helps them persevere. They create not for rewards that might return to them but primarily because they love a creation and want to see it exist.

"All the great things," said poet Robert Frost, "are done for their own sake."

Focussing on what you love pulls divergent thoughts and behaviours into a simple, easy-to-grasp way to transcend life's messiness. Powered by the intensity of love, focus produces a clear image of what you want. A clear, compelling vision of a result you desire acts as an organizing force. It helps you align your values, see what is relevant in current reality, and organize your actions in support of what you want to create.

Creating is not just an individual act. By acting with the force of love — for each other and for what they want to create — couples can *co-create* what matters. Indeed, as Antoine de Saint-Exupéry said in his book, *Wind, Sand, and Stars*, "love does not consist in gazing at each other but in looking outward together in the same direction." However, rather than simply being with reality as it is and putting energy and effort into envisioning and creating what they most want, many couples do exactly the opposite. They focus on problems, argue about the "right" solutions, and erode the love between them. That's what Celia and Al were doing until Al was struck by the power of his love for Celia. As they focussed on their love for each other, it became more complex, fuller, and deeper; their relationship became simpler, richer, and more fulfilling. They clarified personal visions of what they each wanted in their own lives. Then they co-created a vision of the relationship they wanted to create. "Tapping into the power of love," Celia said, "took us a long way towards crafting the simplicity on the other side of complexity."

Simple Enough for What?

From a creator's point of view, complexity is not the enemy. It is the essential raw material of creating. It is something to embrace and work with as you create the simple yet rich order on the other side. The result is a simplicity that is simple enough, but no simpler. However, that begs the question, "Simple enough for what?"

Richard Gregg explored this question in his 1936 article "Voluntary Simplicity," which was reprinted in *Co-Evolution Quarterly* just as the previous simple living wave crested in 1977. Gregg's definition of simplicity is, I think, the most comprehensive and inspiring description of the simplicity on the other side of complexity. It contains essential clues about how to engage the messiness of life and navigate through it toward what truly matters.

"Simplicity," said Gregg, "involves both inner and outer conditions. It means singleness of purpose, sincerity, and honesty within as well as avoidance of exterior clutter, of many possessions irrelevant to the chief purpose of life. It means an ordering and guiding of our energy and our desires, a partial restraint in some directions in order to secure a greater abundance of life in other directions. It involves a deliberate organization of life for a purpose."

Gregg understood that to simplify is to unify, to make whole. Living simply was for him a strategy for "ordering and guiding" his energy, desires, and actions around a *purpose.* Simplifying for Gregg was not about moving away from things but about moving toward what he loved and wanted to see exist, an "abundance of life." Like a sculptor, he carved away what was extraneous to his purpose, not because he saw it as a problem to solve, but rather because it enabled him to focus on and express the essential form of his own simple yet abundant life.

Gregg's purpose was to create a life of purpose. For him, that was to practice, reflect on, and write about the benefits of the simple, contemplative life. He also knew that each of us must discover for ourselves what we love enough to create. Each of us must craft our own answer to the question *Simple enough for what?* Our challenge is to craft our own purpose, to envision a life that supports it, and then wrap the diverse parts of our lives around that vision so that all our actions consistently support what matters.

Unfortunately, most of us do not live such passionate, love-driven, and integrated lives. An American philosopher, Michael Polyani, I think, suggested that most of us go through life doing what is second or third most important to us. By this, I think he meant that we focus on lesser desires such as status, fame, and financial success because we're afraid to risk failing at what we truly love. We pursue those lesser desires hoping that by achieving them we will get the higher things we really care about: love, respect, freedom, creativity, connectedness, and contentment. Either way, what matters most is left undone. The fact that we fail by omission seems to escape us. As does the self-respect and satisfaction that come from doing and creating what we love.

Richard Gregg clearly understood the connection between simplicity, self-respect, and satisfaction. "We cannot have deep and enduring satisfaction, happiness or joy," he wrote, "unless we have self-respect." He believed that self-respect underlay all higher morality. "We cannot have self-respect," he said, "unless our lives are an earnest attempt to express the finest and most enduring values that we are able to appreciate. Therefore simplicity is an important condition for permanent satisfaction with life." Simplicity was not sacrifice for Gregg. His was not a surface simplicity of mere clutter clearing. On the contrary, his deeper simplicity resulted from arranging his life structures so that his surface behaviour expressed what he most cared about, his finest and most enduring values. His approach to simplicity brought him the joy and satisfaction that comes from pursuing a life of purpose in an integral, focussed way.

Embracing Complexity, Creating Simplicity

I know people who've crafted simple lives that express their finest values and bring them great joy. Twenty years ago, Marla, another frustrated teacher, struggled with "the system." When she asked to teach part-time, she was refused. Frustrated by the trade-off between the comfortable security of full-time teaching and the risky, but deep desire to be a writer, she took the plunge. She quit teaching, cut her expenses, worked part time in a bookstore, and focussed almost all of her attention on a novel that she felt called to write and publish.

"My life didn't get easier when I simplified," she told me over coffee one afternoon at a street cafe near the restored cottage she shares with her partner and a young daughter. "In some ways it got harder. Focussing full-time on writing was much more complex than working for a living, but it was a complexity I accepted and enjoyed. I never felt like I sacrificed."

She paused and looked out at the cars passing on the street outside. She turned back to me and continued. "I guess it's because I *chose* that complexity, rather than had it forced on me. No matter how hard the writing process got, I always knew I was focussed on something larger than my self, something worth all the effort. And that made the hard things easier. It kept me going." She leaned forward with an intense, questioning look in her eyes. "Does that make sense?" she asked. "Yes," I said. "It does."

Marla isn't famous yet but she does well as a writer and teacher of writing workshops. Her success could have gone to her head, changing her in ways that were not authentic. It could have made her life more complex. Stewart Brand, founder and first editor of *The Co-Evolution Quarterly*, remarked that, "There's a couple of hazards in Voluntary Simplicity. One is arrogance. Another is success (artistic, commercial, personal) which leads to temptations which lead back again to Involuntary Complexity — too much going on to do anything right."[16] That didn't happen to Marla. Because she'd voluntarily engaged complexity, she kept writing the kinds of novels she wanted to write and living the life that she felt best supported her work. "Once I got my focus clear," she said, "the rest of it just kind of fell into place."

As we left the cafe, Marla stopped, touched my arm, and said, "Living simply is not just about being frugal. For me, it's mostly about freedom. I need to focus on what speaks to me, to write in a way that my readers and I both respect. It's also about wholeness and authenticity. By letting go of what's not essential and focussing on what truly matters, I feel my life is fuller, more authentic, and whole. The richness and satisfaction I get from living with such focus more than makes up for any loss of luxury. I feel very good about myself and my life."

I smiled and nodded. We started walking again. Marla, like Richard Gregg, clearly understood the critical connection between simplicity, self-respect, and satisfaction.

What's Driving the Action?

To be able to express our "finest and most enduring values," we need to clarify our motives and their relationships to each other. Knowing what motivates us helps us understand the structure of our lives. If you are driven by short-term demands, for example, your life will be different than if you were driven by a desire for lasting results. Knowing your motives helps you recognize the forces in play. Aware of those forces, it's easier to deliberately create life structures that integrate simplicity and success and move you toward what matters. If you long to be the architect of your own life, but discover that you habitually react or respond to life's challenges as problems, don't despair. By recognizing that pattern, you are halfway to success. Seeing the pattern enables you to transcend it. You have the option to approach life's messiness from a reactive, problem-solving stance *or* from a results-focussed, creative stance. You can fight it or embrace it. However, knowing that you have that choice greatly increases your power to influence the course and shape of your own life.

I know a finishing carpenter, Brent, who has lived this way since the mid-seventies. A Buddhist, he chooses to live near the poverty line in a luxuriously wood-paneled school bus in a small tourist town. He takes pride in his craftsmanship. His reputation for quality allows him to choose when and for whom he works. Brent's results are so exquisite that an upscale couple recently paid him $25,000 to build them a kitchen. "That'll get me through the year," Brent told me. "If another interesting project comes up, I'll think about it seriously, but I've got lots I want to do if it doesn't. I might drive the bus to Mexico and hang out for a few months. Maybe I'll do a little writing. And, of course, there's always my Buddhist practice."

The couple for whom he built the kitchen were as impressed with the simplicity of Brent's way of life as they were with the beautiful work he'd done. "I envy that simplicity," one of them told me. "Watching him work, listening to him describe how he lives, made me think. I mean, I like this kitchen, but while he's sipping margaritas and sleeping in his own bed beside a Mexican beach, I'll be busting my hump at a job I don't really care about any more, just to pay for all this." He paused, chuckled to himself, then added, "Something's not quite right here."

Brent loves beautiful things. He makes his living hand crafting beautiful things for others. But money and things do not drive his actions. The deep values of his faith, his daily practice, and his vision of a simple yet fulfilling life are the forces that drive his life. "Underlying it all," he told me, "is choice. Even when things are tough, I can fall back on the fact that no one forces me to live this way. I chose it. And I keep choosing it."

Brent's and Marla's lives are no less messy than others' are. Both own a minimum of material things and sometimes wish they had more. Both live close to what many consider poverty and worry about slipping over into *involuntary* simplicity. Both struggle with the complexities of relationships and other challenges. Both flirt with fears that what they're doing is not good enough. However, out of this messiness, both have crafted a simplicity that is rich, authentic, *and* fully engaged. Both have found the place where their passion and the world's hunger intersect. By deliberately focussing on creating what matters to themselves and others, both have crafted a simplicity that is successful, satisfying, *and* enduring. Both live in ways that give them a deep sense that their messy lives are creative, coherent, and fulfilling wholes.

"I'm not always wildly happy," Brent said, "and I'd worry if I was. But I love what I do and I'm definitely content with what I have. Life is good. And that's good enough for me."

From A Middle to A Higher Way

As Celia and Al grasped the differences between the two kinds of simplicity, they began to let go of their need to control or fix their messes. They opened to the riskier but more exciting prospect of dancing with the forces. And it paid off. "Through our work with you," a bright-eyed, smiling Celia told me about a year after we'd finished our sessions, "we learned that problem-solving was a simplistic reaction to what we didn't want. We saw that what we wanted wasn't so much a middle way as a higher way. Now, simplifying lets us organize the bits and pieces of our life around our highest values. For us, that means arranging our business and management skills so they support our social and environmental goals. Getting involved with the Sustainability Group was the best thing we ever did, personally and professionally."

"We wanted simple yet purposeful, engaged lives," added Alverjo, looking relaxed and energetic. "But problem-solving didn't do it. Our lives felt like scattered, unfocussed heaps. Now, we're focussed on creating what matters. We hardly ever focus on problems, and when we do, we make sure solutions support the big picture results we want. It works. It's gratifying to finally figure out how to simplify and how to succeed at exciting, challenging work. I'm proud of how we live now. It's like we have it all." They smiled, then Celia added, "Now, all we have to do is learn is how to not sound like you when we explain this to our friends." We laughed, and through the sparkle in their eyes, I thought I could see a dancing star emerging.

A Caveat: You Can't Change What You Don't Acknowledge

I'd love to tell you that all it takes to create a simple, successful life is read this book or attend one of my workshops, but I'd be lying. Creating takes as long to master as other complex skills such as skiing or playing the piano. Although clients make changes quickly, most take from six months to two years of focussed practice before they can consistently create what matters most. That so many succeed gives me hope that, with mastery of the skills and framework of creating, all of us — simple-livers, downshifters, and the rest of us — can *create* the lives, work, relationships, and communities, even the world that we long for.

However, a caveat is in order. After twenty-five years of helping would-be creators, I have found that the most difficult hurdle they confront is the habit of focussing on problems. I've discovered that *before* they can fully embrace the creative process, they must recognize the limits of problem-solving. Those who rush into the creative process before they fully understand problem-solving's flaws inevitably try to force their new creating skills into their old problem-focussed framework. So, before we look more deeply into the creative process, I ask that you be patient while we explore the structure and limits of problem-solving. Understanding how problem-focussed life structures can work *against* your dreams and desires will help you appreciate the structures you will need to create what you most want.

Chapter Five

The Problem with Problem-solving: An Introduction

(Life)…is an action to be performed without rehearsal or respite… it is a mystery, not indeed to be solved but to be restated according to some vision, however imperfect.

Jacques Barzun

Do you ever wake up with your mind swarming with images of problems you "have to" solve? Does an inner *Voice of Judgment* threaten dire consequences if you don't get rid of the complexity swirling around you? Do you feel guilty or hopeless about what you're *not* able to do? Maybe not, but that's how many of my problem-focussed clients tell me they wake up.

To motivate themselves, they fight fire with fire. They conjure up frightening visions of what might happen if they *don't* solve their problems, and then react to those negative scenarios. "I'll get fired if I don't get the report done right away." "My spouse will hate me if I don't clean out the garage." "Everyone will laugh at me if I don't lose 20 pounds before the reunion." Using negative visions to scare themselves into action, they spend their days focussed on what they don't like and don't want. They dissipate precious life energy trying to get rid of (or get relief from) the fear, anxiety, anger, and depression that come from focussing so intently on problems. They have little time or energy left for actions that would move them toward what they want. Most do not even have time to clarify or envision *what* they want.

At the end of the day, these folks are stressed, frustrated, and worn out. At the end of many such days, they feel helpless, depressed, and anxious. Although this might not be the way most of us live, it is, I think, a good description of what Thoreau meant when he said that the mass of us lead lives of quiet desperation. Whether we live like this on a daily basis or just when things get difficult, framing our lives as a never-end-ing struggle against problems is neither a healthy nor productive way to live. Why, then, are so many hooked on problem-solving?

Convergent Problems; Divergent Challenges

It's said that to a person with a hammer, everything looks like a nail.

Similarly, to those who rely on problem-solving, almost everything looks like a problem. Problem-solving is what we're taught to do. It's our culture's predominant way of producing results. Besides, most of us lack the expertise to *create* what we *most* want. Robert Fritz, only partly tongue in cheek, sums up the reasons for this in the title of his book for teenagers, *A Short Course In Creating What You Always Wanted To But Couldn't Because Nobody Ever Told You How Because They Didn't Know Either*.[17] So, unaware of the *creating* option and hooked into our problem-solving habits, we frame difficult, challenging, and complex situations as *problems* that can and must be solved. But most of those challenge are *not* problems and *not* solvable.

In *A Guide for the Perplexed*, E.F. Schumacher points out that there are two fundamentally different kinds of questions or challenges that we call "problems."[18] The first, which he calls *convergent* problems, narrow down to *single* solutions. The more intelligently you study them, the more the answers converge around that one solution.

QUESTION / PROBLEM  **ANSWERS/ RESULTS**

This kind of problem *is* solvable. Ask thirty experts what the solution is to a broken tibia bone or a malfunctioning dishwasher and they will give you basically the same answer. However, ask thirty experts, "What is the best way to raise children, run a country, or craft a simple yet successful life?" and you're likely to get thirty different answers. Questions like this are *divergent*. They are open-ended and messy. The more you study them, the more the answers diverge from each other.

**QUESTION /
CHALLENGE**   **ANSWERS/
RESULTS**

Divergent questions are not problems that *can* be solved. They are challenges to be grappled with, mysteries to be pondered, questions to be lived with. Divergent questions don't have a "correct" answer. They do not lend themselves to straight-line logic and simplistic "solutions." In fact, the more we try to clarify and solve them logically, the more they diverge. If we push them to extremes we end up with pairs of conflicting opposites, dichotomies such as "Freedom *vs.* Discipline," "Growth *vs.* Decay," "Dependence *vs.* Independence," or "Simplicity *vs.* Success."

Schumacher says that it is important to recognize these pairs of opposites although our logical mind doesn't like them. It prefers the simplistic yes/no logic of computers. "So," he says, "at any time it wishes to give its exclusive allegiance to either or the other of the pair ... the mind may suddenly change sides, often without noticing it." Downshifters suddenly upshift; simplifiers become upscale consumers. Every time the mind "swings like a pendulum from one opposite to the other," Schumacher adds, "it feels as if you are "making up your mind afresh." At other times, he says that the mind may become rigid and lifeless, fixing itself on one side of the pair of opposites and feeling that the problem has been solved. Either way, because we fail to see both sides of the challenge, our solutions merely produce partial, temporary results.

Most of the difficult situations we face — large or small — are *not* convergent problems. They are messy, open-ended, divergent challenges. Rather than flail away at such challenges with our problem-solving hammers, there are more useful ways to approach them.

The first is suggested by the poet Rainer Maria Rilke in "Letters to a Young Poet:"

> Be patient toward all that is unsolved in your heart and try to love the questions themselves.... Do not now seek the answers, which cannot be given you because you would not be able to live them. And the point is, to live everything. Live the ques-

tions now. Perhaps you will then gradually, without noticing it, live along some distant day into the answer.[19]

But *how* do we live those questions?

Divergent questions and challenges put tension into the world and into our lives. Although such tension is neither good nor bad, our logical minds want to remove it by coming down on one side or the other of the pair of opposites. We saw earlier that when you try to *solve* dichotomies by coming down on one side, the other side cries out for resolution. The tension is shifted, not resolved. Action in such a structure oscillates between divergent poles. Instead of focussing on either pole of a divergent question, or trying to balance the two, we can transcend the polarity. By using the *creative* tension that arises out of "living the questions," we can shift our focus to a higher level.

Transcending Tension

Divergent challenges can be transcended by going beyond problem-solving. Schumacher's pairs of opposites "cease to be opposites," he says, "at the higher level, the really human level, where self-awareness plays its proper role." At the level of the whole person, higher, more senior forces such as love, compassion, truth, understanding, and creativity enable us to embrace and transcend these polar opposites. Schumacher gives the slogan of the French Revolution as an example. "To the pair of opposites, *Liberté* and *Egalité*, irreconcilable in ordinary logic, [they] added a third factor or force — *Fraternité*, brotherliness — which comes from a higher level." With too much freedom, the strong overpower the weak. However, to enforce equality we have to restrict freedom. The values conflict unless transcended by the higher order force of *human caring* that Schumacher calls "brotherliness." Whereas freedom and equality can be legislated, caring, he says, comes only from "individual persons mobilizing their own higher forces and faculties."

The creative process is more powerful than problem-solving — and simpler — because it mobilizes such higher forces. By tapping into the forces of love and truth, we can transcend emotional tension and establish creative tension. Working with creative tension, we can transcend problem-solving in favour of creating what matters.

The Urge to Create

Carl Jung recognized the wisdom in transcending divergent challenges when he said that life's most important problems are not solved, only outgrown. They fade away when confronted with a new and stronger life urge. Perhaps the most powerful life urge we experience is the urge to create. *Creating* is driven by the power of love, it is rooted in the truth of current reality, and it expresses our creative spirit through playful yet focussed action. Most important, the structure of creating embraces the kind of hierarchy of values that Schumacher describes above, a hierarchy in which more important values guide the expression of less important values. Creating embraces the tension of opposites. It uses creative tension as a source of energy with which to transcend conflict and to produce what matters.

When we master our own creative process, we find it easier to be patient with all that is unsolved and to love the questions. However, until we do, we often find ourselves merely reacting to what happens, responding to the intensity of problems, issues, and circumstances. Such action is not likely to produce the results we want to create. It's more likely to distract than to empower us.

The Illusion of Success

In *The Path of Least Resistance,* Robert Fritz says:

> Problem solving provides an almost automatic way of organizing your focus, actions, time, and thought processes. In a sense, when you have a nice juicy problem to work on, you do not have to think. You can obsess instead. ... Problem solving can be very distracting while at the same time giving you the illusion that you are doing something important and needed.

This morning, for example, I heard a news item about miners protesting mine closures. Faced with the fear of a jobless future and the loss of a life-long sense of identity, one miner lapsed into deep depression. He stayed sick until his union decided to fight the closures. Describing how that decision snapped her husband out of his depression, the miner's wife said, "I don't think he or the union have a hope in hell. But I don't care if he's right or wrong. I don't care if this works or not. At least *for now* he *feels* like a man."

Because problem-solving distracts us, it disempowers us. When we react to circumstances, the power is not in our own hands. It's *outside* — in circumstances. Desperately seeking control, we feel we must constantly react to events and situations that happen to us. As Celia and Alverjo experienced, the lives of those who rely on problem-solving become overly complicated and fragmented. Hooked on problem-solving, obsessed with immediate relief, they are often left frustrated, helpless, and even hopeless. They become victims of circumstances.

Problem-solving is always a tempting option because it *is* sometimes the perfect strategy. It works well in convergent situations. In divergent situations, however, it merely gives us the *illusion* of working well. That's why it fails to provide a solid foundation on which to create the successful simplicity on the other side of complexity. To create that simplicity, we must express our creative urge. In the creative process, the actions we take are not reactions to circumstances. They are strategic steps designed to bring into being the results we truly want to create.

When you master the workings of your own creative process, you are able to choose *problem-solving* to deal with convergent problems and *creating* to deal with divergent ones. As your skills and capacity to create become more complex, your life will become simpler, easier to manage, and more satisfying. The key to letting go of your reliance on problem-solving is to understand when and where it fits as a useful tool and where it doesn't. Before we turn to the creative process, let's examine why problem-solving fails to provide a solid foundation on which to create the life we long for.

Problem-Solving: A Shaky Foundation for Creating A Future

A deep, fulfilling, and sustainable simplicity is like a well-built house, only as solid and enduring as its foundation. The foundations of our lives depend on how we structure the relationships between elements such as ideas, values, beliefs, aspirations, and day-to-day reality. Some structures are like sailboats; they move toward results and stay there. Other structures are like rocking chairs; they move back and forth. Problem-solving's structure oscillates. It moves first toward then away from the results you want to create.

Flaws in Problem-solving Approaches

Six flaws prevent problem-solving from consistently producing real and lasting results:

1. We mistakenly apply convergent approaches to divergent challenges.
2. Focussing on problems depresses people, often leaving them sullen and pouty.
3. The energy it takes to pout is not available to create results.
4. Most problem-solving is focussed on relief, not lasting results.
5. The cure can be worse than the disease; shortsighted solutions become new problems.
6. The structure of problem-solving generates actions and results that oscillate between better and worse. It does not support the creation of real and lasting results.

Understanding why and how these limitations play out in our lives can help us unhook from our problem-solving habit and open ourselves more fully to creating.

1. We mistakenly apply convergent solutions to divergent challenges.

As we saw above, we often apply problem-solving to divergent challenges that are neither "problems" nor solvable. As Celia and Alverjo discovered, when we come down on one side of a dichotomy such as *simplicity* vs. *success*, the other cries out for resolution. Moving toward simplicity increases the desire for success; striving for success leaves us longing for simplicity. The tension is not resolved, just shifted. Although such divergent challenges cannot be solved, they can, as we shall see, be transcended.

2. Focussing on problems depresses people.

Recall the exercise you did at the beginning of the book — the one in which you imagined your worst problem and focussed on it? Remember how negatively you felt when you focussed on that problem? Down? Stuck? Depressed?

It's not just individuals who are shocked when I tell them that problem-solving is neither the best nor only way to produce lasting results. Business owners, managers, executives, and the organizational and community leaders who take part in my *Strategic Design* workshops also stare skeptically at me when I challenge the long-term practicality of problem-solving.

However, once I describe the work of Ronald Lippitt, they lean forward with interest. Together with Kurt Lewin (the father of "field theory"), Lippitt coined the term "group dynamics" in the 1940's. His research, described by Marvin Weisbord in *Discovering Common Ground*,[20] showed, that "listing and solving problems depresses groups." Lippitt, says Weisbord, was "appalled to hear people in his groups using words like "hopeless," "frustrating," and "impotent" as they applied some of his own group methods to problem-solving." He saw that much of the focus of his groups was on seeking relief from anxiety, *not* on producing lasting results. Worse, the relief they sought was in part from the pain that came from listing and focussing on problems. Fifty years ago, Lippitt discovered something that therapists, counselors, business consultants, community leaders, and myriad's of self-help authors and practitioners have not fully recognized or have chosen to ignore — *focussing on problems depresses people.*

Once he recognized the negative effects of his problem-focussed strategies, Lippitt changed his approach to increase rather than drain energy from his clients. Weisbord says that he focussed them on 'images of potential' — envisioning what could be instead of lamenting what was. Working with systems expert Edward Lindaman, who directed planning for the Apollo moon mission, Lippitt showed that a vision of a "preferred future" was a more powerful motivator than problem-solving. "Lippitt and Lindaman found that when people plan present actions by working backwards from what is really desired, they developed energy, enthusiasm, optimism, and high commitment."[21]

Despite the success of future-focussed projects such as the Apollo Mission, most business, health care, and self-help experts still focus clients on problems and solutions. However, visionaries like Robert Fritz and David Cooperrider, an advocate of the "Appreciative Inquiry" approach, have challenged the effectiveness of problem-solving.

"We have reached "the end of problem-solving," says Cooperrider. It is not, he says, "a mode of inquiry capable of inspiring, mobilizing, and sustaining human system change."

The future, he and Fritz assert, belongs to those with the capacity to create what matters.

3. The energy it takes to pout is not available for creating results.

Many of my clients, frustrated by their failure to solve persisting problems and their inability to create the results they most want, begin to resent their own lives. They become sullen and withdrawn, blaming circumstances, other people, or forces outside themselves for their failures. They see themselves as victims of circumstance and start to pout. Pouting is a way to manipulate others into feeling sorry for you when things aren't going the way you'd like them to go. Frustrated clients pout because they're depressed and don't know what to do. Not only is it depressing to focus on problems, it is *doubly* depressing to invest time, energy, and effort doing so only to find that solving problems does not produce the results you want. The irony is that pouting is another problem-solving strategy. It, too, fails to produce real and lasting results. In fact, it makes pouters feel worse. Moreover, pouting is a form of pessimism, and pessimism is one of the prime causes of depression. Depression saps energy and erodes your inclination to act. It's a vicious circle. When things were not going well for her and Al, Celia told me that they knew they were pouting and knew that it produced a vicious circle, but they didn't know how to stop. I suggested they reverse that circle by shifting their focus to creating.

Duke Ellington captured the essence of the shift from a depressing, problem-driven focus to the energizing, future-focussed stance of the creator when he said, "I took the energy it takes to pout and wrote blues tunes with it." The Duke's soulful tunes were not solutions to problems. They were expressions of his spirit, acts of creation performed in spite of the problems he faced and the pain he felt. Ellington's courageous stance acknowledged his problems and embraced their energy. Then he transcended his problems by creating songs of great power and reach. Though sometimes sad, always soulful, the Duke's blues tunes lift listeners, as they lifted him, above sorrow, grief, and depression. They are true creations, his gifts to the world.

All of us have the potential to "take the energy it takes to pout" and create results with it. However, stuck in problem-solving and focussed on relief, many of us don't realize that potential. Worse, when we don't, we judge ourselves as failing, which only adds to our sense of helplessness. Indeed, over-relying on problem-solving often results in a downward spiral into despair and a deep sense of hopelessness about the future.

4. Most problem-solving is focussed on relief, not results.

Most problem-solving is driven more by a desire to reduce the intensity of problems than by a desire to produce real and lasting results. In most cases, action is not taken until the intensity (the anxiety, pain, conflict, anger, etc... associated with the problem) is so bad that it compels the problem-solver to take action. We've all experienced the irritating but bearable tooth that should be looked at, but gets put off because of lack of time or money or an aversion to dentistry. Or we've faced the ever-increasing clutter that depresses us and threatens to drown us in stuff, but is not yet bad enough to warrant a change of priorities or a major house cleaning. However, when the problem's intensity rises to the point where the pain or the clutter is no longer bearable, the problem solver reacts with action designed to reduce that intensity. Now!

Often, however, the action taken only reduces the intensity of the symptoms and does not result in a long-term solution. Nor does it result in what we truly want coming into being.

Because problem-solving focuses on *intensity*, it merely produces temporary relief. Taking aspirin provides relief from a stress headache but does not change the structure that caused the stress-producing behaviour. Instead, the relief it produces allows us to keep doing what causes the stress and pain. When the drug wears off, the problem reoccurs. We're back where we started, or worse, well on our way to ulcers. Trying to solve the stress yields the same pattern. Relieving stress without changing the structure that gives rise to it allows us to keep doing what causes it. Research shows that stress management programs can turn chronic burnout into acute break-down by teaching people to cope with ever-increasing amounts of stress until they break.

Most solutions driven by a need for relief eventually lead to worse problems.

5. The cure is often worse than the disease.

Not only does problem-solving fail to fix problems, it often inten-sifies them. As with aspirin and stomach distress, the cure becomes worse than the disease. British researchers found that building new motorways leads to more drivers and worse congestion. The automo-bile itself was first touted as "the solution to pollution" caused by Victorian horses. A study by the conservative, right wing Rand Institute on the results of the Drug Enforcement Agency's war against drugs concluded that the "ultimate activity was to increase the profit margin on cocaine, increase the incentive for dealers and thereby increase rather than decrease the traffic in crack."[22]

Systems thinkers call such results "counter-intuitive effects of naïve intervention." They result from applying narrow, problem-solving, relief focussed techniques to complex, open-ended challenges that do not lend themselves to narrow, specific solutions. This has serious implications for simplicity seekers. Naïvely seeking relief from the stress of complexity by simplifying can lead to lack of challenge, boredom, and a renewed long-ing for comforts and conveniences. Celia and Al's country-living cure for stress became their biggest problem.

6. Problem-solving oscillates between better then worse.

Problem-solving rests on a foundation—a structure or framework—in which energy and action tend to oscillate between better and worse. The "solutions" it generates rarely move toward final, completed results. During a *Simplicity and Success* workshop, Celia and Alverjo discovered the structure that gave rise to their frustrating oscillation. "It's like we held two versions of success in mind at the same time," said Al. "Satisfying one version increased a desire for the other. Satisfying the other left us longing for what we missed from the first."

When two values compete, a kind of *structural conflict* is created.[23]

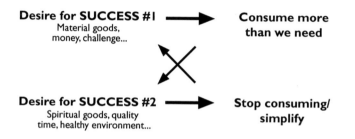

In this, as in any structure, energy and action flow where it is easiest to go. As the desire for Success #1 is satisfied, the desire for Success # 2 increases. As you shift your focus to Success #2, the desire for Success #1 increases. The natural tendency — the path of least resistance — in this structure is for energy and action to oscillate back and forth between consumption and simplification. You cannot "solve" this *structural* conflict by denying or deleting either value. Deleting values is *not* possible. We want what we want — *all* of it. Our minds are not machines from which we can delete unwanted desires without diminishing the complexity that gives rise to our humanness. Pretending that you don't value what you do value leads only to the simplicity on *this* side of complexity.

You can, however, create a structure in which you satisfy both desires, a structure that overcomes all the flaws that prevent problem-solving from producing lasting results.

The Structure of Success

Changing the *relationship* between competing desires changes the structure. Doing so sets up a path of least resistance in which energy and action move toward your most important values. Celia and Al *integrated* their two versions of success by arranging them in the structure of the creative process. When they did, it looked something like this:

PRIMARY CHOICE: SUCCESS #1

(Spiritual goods, quality time,
health, sustainable environment...)

Organize
SECONDARY CHOICE: SUCCESS #2
(Material goods, money, challenge...)
so that it suports Success #1

In this structure, Success #1 becomes primary; it drives the action. Once Celia and Al prioritized their values, they reshaped their definition of success so that pursuing it also supported their higher order values of simplicity, ecological health, and spirituality. Such structural change is the key that enables simple-livers to transcend the trade-off between conflicting values and to consistently produce real and lasting results.

Structure Gives Rise to Behaviour

Structure refers to how the pieces and parts of a system are put together, to the *relationship* between the parts. Just as heap of bicycle parts is not a bicycle until those parts are connected properly, the structure of our own lives depends on the way we arrange our values, aspirations, beliefs, fears, and day-to-day reality itself.

If we arrange our values in "either/or" structures, our actions are likely to oscillate between one value then the other. Although we may achieve a temporary "balance" by arranging values in a "both/and" structure, that structure, like a child's seesaw, is inherently unstable. Provoked by adversity, it quickly shifts to an oscillating structure. Balance is not the way to integrate simplicity and success. Celia and Al transcended their conflicting values by aligning them hierarchically so that lower level values and actions supported higher level values and aspirations. Within such a hierarchy of values, we can satisfy all our values without significantly detracting from any of them.

Understanding the structural limits of problem-solving helped Celia and Alverjo realize why their well-intended efforts had not produced the kind and quality of results they longed for. "We were too problem-focussed," said Celia, "too concerned about getting rid of what we did *not* want. We rarely took action to move us toward what we *did* want."

"Once we saw why problem-solving and balance-seeking fail to produce consistent results," said Alverjo, "we were ready to explore a new approach, a new structure."

That structure is the structure of *creating*.

Creating the Future We Most Want

As more people realize that *creating* is the key to producing the purposeful, lasting change they long for, a deep shift in the structure of our individual and collective lives becomes possible. In this shift to a creation-focussed approach, conformity gives way to creativity. Dependence and independence give way to autonomous interdependence. Self-help gives way to self-creation. Consumption gives way to creativity. In a creation-focussed approach, simple living becomes less about sacrifice and more about creating authentic, fully engaged lives. It becomes a process of focussing on what matters, accepting what is, and then aligning action and energy so that what you do supports what you want.

The future does not just unfold; we create it each day, each moment, by what we envision, choose, and do. Within the rapidly changing, increasingly complex context of post-modern life, people are discovering and embracing the power of the creative process. They are discovering that problem-solving is a limited way to produce results, that it leads to the simplicity on this side of complexity. Only *creating* leads to the simplicity on the other side of complexity.

"Those who do not create the future they want," cautions Draper L. Kaufman in *Systems One*, "must endure the future they get."[24] By mastering the skills and practices of creating and by applying them in our lives, work, and relationships, each of us can significantly increase our chances of bringing into being the lives we so deeply long for.

To start our exploration of the creative process, we'll first look at some of the superficial approaches to "creativity" that are promoted in self-help and business development workshops. Then we'll compare those surface level approaches to the deeper, more powerful, and enduring approach with which creators have always brought creations into being.

Chapter Six

Creativity? Or Creating Results?

*Because simplicity seems easy we believe it is easy to
achieve. When it is not easy to achieve we give up too
quickly. Simplicity is easy to use but can be hard to
design. You may need some creativity.*

Edward de Bono

"But," argued Alverjo in one of our coaching sessions, "both of us
are *already* creative."

He was responding to my suggestion that he and Celia take part
in a *Simplicity and Success* workshop. I thought doing so might help
them develop the structure and skills needed to create the kind and
quality of life they aspired to.

"Our jobs demand that we think creatively," he pressed. "In fact,
it sometimes seems that all we do is sit around in meetings, brainstorming new ideas and approaches." He crossed his arms across his
chest, then added, "We don't need *more* creativity stuff."

"It's true," added Celia, leaning forward and patting Al's leg.
"We're always trying new ways at work, doing things differently. It's
exhausting! We have a whole shelf of books and tapes on creativity,
and both of us have taken a bunch of courses on thinking outside the
box."

"It's obvious that you are both creative *thinkers*," I agreed. "But
didn't you come to me because, in spite of your ability to brainstorm
and think outside the box, you have not yet been able to put your
ideas into practice, to actually create the results you want?"

"Yes?" said Alverjo, grinning, wary now of my questioning style.

"Do you think that, as well as creative thinking skills, you might
also need to master the skills of creative *doing*?"

"I suppose," said Celia, nodding her head. Alverjo scrunched up
his face like a chess player who just realized he'd put himself in check.
Then he smiled again.

"There is," I suggested, "a radical difference between *being* creative and actually *creating* the results you want. Before you too quickly dismiss *creating's* practicality, let's take a deeper look at that difference."

Creativity *or* Creating?

The word "create" comes from the Latin *creare*, meaning to produce, to make. My *Compact Oxford English Dictionary* defines "create" as "to bring into being, cause to exist, esp. to produce where nothing was before, 'to form out of nothing'." There is no entry in my four thousand-page Oxford for "creativity," but the *Concise Oxford* defines it as "inventive and imaginative." Most people I ask define it as "doing things differently."

The word "creativity" refers more often to style than substance, as in the case of an advertising account executive complaining that "we need more creativity in this approach." What often passes for creativity is merely the same old stuff dressed up in a new package. In the corporate world, creativity is often an add-on, something imaginative or inventive that is sprinkled on after the fact to "spice up" a product or service.

Creators are sometimes — but not always — creative in the way they bring things into being. They may think imaginatively or inventively. They may come up with unusual things. Mozart, for example, envisioned and heard complete symphonies in his head while out walking and then went home and wrote them out in ink. His composition books are pristine. Other creators are more linear and conventional in their approach. Beethoven's notebooks are black masses of scribbles and corrections. He laboured long and hard to craft his majestic works, even using a slide rule to work out the mathematics of his harmonics. Still others, like experimental performance artists, can be wildly unconventional, imaginative, and improvisational. Most creators, however, combine a variety of approaches, seeking whatever process best serves the result — the creation — they want to bring into being.

The drive to create — the deep, persistent urge to bring into being something that you'd love to see exist — is different from creativity. The drive to create says Stephen Nachmanovitch, sets creators apart from individuals who are merely creative.

"The drive to create ... characterizes someone who is driven to do something from the depths, something that he or she feels must be done regardless of whether it's popular or well rewarded by society. This inner compulsion to realize a vision depends on creativity for its fulfillment, but it is not the same as creativity. The inspired poet or musician may in fact be less creative, less clever, adept, or original than the designer of an advertising campaign, but he is motivated by a life-or-death need to bring the vision into being."[25]

Although creativity is often an important component of creating, it is a mistake to see it as the whole of the creative process. You rarely, for example, see groups of painters, sculptors, or poets "brainstorming" different ways to approach their canvas, stone, or blank page. And when you do, such as when aspiring writers workshop a new piece, or musicians "jam", it's just one of many steps, not the whole process of creating.

Because of its association with doing things differently, creativity is often confused with the unusual, unconventional, or the outright bizarre. In a creativity course that Robert Fritz told me about, participants dressed up in chicken suits and jumped around making clucking noises to help them "free their creative spirit." Other popular approaches to creativity recommend that you whack or kick yourself (metaphorically, of course) in vulnerable body parts. Can you imagine Margaret Atwood clucking like a chicken? Or Georgia O'Keefe? I doubt that Robert Frost whacked himself upside the head to shake loose the lines in "The Road Not Taken."

Although creators do come up with imaginative processes and unusual results from time to time, *the unusual is not the essence of the creative process*. Though some will dispute this assertion, a creator's end result is usually predictable. A novelist usually ends up with a novel, a painter with a painting. Architects see buildings take shape as they were envisioned. Although the path may vary from straight to crooked, from up and down to a rising spiral, the essence of the creative process is that it leads step-by-step to the outcome desired by the creator.

You can see this complex combination of predictability and creativity by comparing Picasso's original sketch for his famous painting *Guernica* with the painting itself. Picasso knew what he wanted to achieve; the sketch contains much of the final form. However, the finished painting includes great detail that the painter worked out through a progression of sketches and studies. "Picasso," says John Briggs in *Fire in the Crucible*, "was not stating a contradiction but plain fact when he said that a picture 'remains almost intact' from its first inspiration and yet 'is not thought out and settled beforehand.'"[26]

Even those who insist that their creating is unplanned and spontaneous usually end up with predictable results. For example, a poet in a college workshop I did claimed she *never* wrote with any end in mind. "I can't," she told us, "It would stifle my creativity."

"So how do you create a poem?" someone asked her.

"I just go quiet and it comes to me," she said. "Then I write it down."

"But," I asked, "isn't *it* inevitably a poem? Not a novel. Not an essay. Not a ceramic pot or a screenplay. Isn't *it* always, predictably, a poem?"

"Yes," she said cautiously, then added, "but each poem is amazingly different."

"Fair enough," I said, " but isn't a poem what you set out to produce when you go quiet? Isn't a poem the end, the final form, that you have in mind when you write *it* down?"

"Well, yes," she reluctantly agreed, "I guess it is."

"So," I asked, "would it be fair to say that you intentionally create a space — a framework or a field of possibilities — in which poems can spontaneously come to you?"

"Ah!" she said, smiling as if a light had gone on inside her head, "That *is* what I do."

A Fundamentally Different Approach

Creating is a powerful process because not only does it generate surprise and novelty, but also because it leads reliably to the end results envisioned by a creator. When someone asks, "How can I live my life, do my work, or produce my product more creatively?" they miss the point. The question implies that creativity is a kind of magic pill you take to make things better. Such an approach smacks strongly of problem-solving. However, creating is not about fixing what doesn't work. Neither is it about merely doing things in stylistically different ways. It is not positive thinking, visualization, or brainstorming (although it might include all of these elements). Moreover, it is not a trendy form of life planning designed to superficially change the *way* you do things. Creating is a fundamentally different way of approaching *what* you do. It is a way of envisioning and then bringing into being what matters; it is a process that embraces and transcends problems, circumstances, and complexity in favour of results you'd love to see exist.

Process *or* Result? Journey *or* Destination?

Integrating simplicity and success is *both* a journey and destination. However, not everyone sees it this way. Many come down on one side or the other of the *process* vs. *results* debate.

"Being in the moment is more important to me than producing results," says a process-focussed workshop participant. "It's the journey that's important not the destination." Another agrees, "I can't see how you can have a planned end and still be spontaneously creative."

Others counter with a "nothing-but-results" approach. "I don't care what I do or how I do it," says a grim-faced participant, "as long as I get where I want to go. It's the end that counts." "Results are everything," says another. "Get them clear and the process will follow."

In this dichotomy, we encounter another of Schumacher's divergent challenges. I have seen couples come apart over this issue. I have seen executive teams struggle over it. I've seen non-profit and community groups stray far from their primary purpose as they engage in endless debates about whether process *or* result is most important. Because this can be a sticking point for many would-be creators, it's worth looking at how to integrate these aspects of creating.

Choosing sides in this (or any) complex dichotomy is a partial and limiting way of viewing reality. Doing so distorts your perception. It prevents you from embracing the whole of the creative act. Successful creators glorify *neither* process *nor* product; they transcend the dichotomy by embracing both without unnecessary attachment.

In his book *Zen and the Art of Motorcycle Maintenance*, writer/philosopher Robert Pirsig described a way to transcend this dilemma. Comparing life's challenges to mountains, he wrote, "Mountains should be climbed with as little effort as possible and without desire. ... To live only for some future goal is shallow. It's the sides of the mountain which sustain life, not the top. Here's where things grow."[27]

"Ha!" exclaim the process defenders. "See!"

However, just when it appears that Pirsig has come down on the side of process, he adds, "But of course, without the top you can't have any sides. It's the top that *defines* the sides." Then, having embraced journey *and* destination, process *and* results, he turns easily, effortlessly, to action. "So on we go . . . no hurry . . . just one step after the next."

There are times in life when being purely in process is appropriate, perhaps during meditation, for example, or making love. Moreover, there are certainly times during the creative process itself when you are totally immersed in process, in "flow." We sometimes put ourselves in process just to experience "flow." This is fine, but it's not necessarily creating. In the creative process, process always serves a creation. Only when you know what you want to create does the question, "What process should I use?" make sense.

Integrating Process *and* Result

When creators honour both process and result, they integrate the rational and the artistic, the intellectual and the actual. They bring their whole self to the creative encounter. Creating is one of the few places in life where the whole person is engaged, where, as Ruskin said about art, the head, hands, and heart come together. By aligning *process* so that it consistently supports desired *results*, creators can give themselves over to that process. They can enter that timeless, joyous flow and still produce the creations for which they most deeply care.

Although creators are usually firm about results, they are also flexible about process. They do not lock themselves into any specific process. If a process does not serve the result they want to produce, they scrap it and try another. I once heard Pam Houston, author of the award-winning book, *Cowboys Are My Weakness,* tell a sold-out audience at the Port Townsend writer's conference that she had just thrown away four hundred and fifty pages of a novel she'd worked on for over a year.

"It wasn't getting me where I wanted to go," she confessed to the stunned audience.

"Was that awful?" someone asked.

"It felt awful," said Houston, "but it wasn't working. So, it had to go."

"What will you do now?" asked the incredulous questioner.

"Start again. Try a new tack," said Houston. "Any more questions?"

Houston did try a new tack. Within a few years she had published *Waltzing the Cat*, a wonderful set of linked fictions that reads more like a novel than a collection of short stories. She also wrote a poignant memoir, *A Little Bit More About Me*, in which she masterfully describes grappling with the challenges of growing into her full self.

"You have to know what you want to get," Gertrude Stein told young writers, "but when you know that, let it take you."[28]

Thinking Outside the Box? Or Creating A New One?

Celia and Al eventually took the workshop I'd suggested. During it, they came to realize that there was much more to creating than just "thinking outside the box."

Much of the confusion that exists between *creating* and *creativity* occurs because most studies about creativity are not about the process and practice of creating. Like most popular courses on creativity, such studies are more about creative *thinking* than doing. Based on theories about how creative people (usually intellectually creative people) *think*, these academic approaches focus more on *preparation* for creating than on *practice*. Consequently, the research fails to address the practical skills and strategies creators use to bring actual creations into being. It has little to do with the *act* of creating. Like humour, creating requires much more than intellect. When comedian Tom Hanks was asked if humour was an intellectual process, he replied, *"No! If it was, intellectuals could do it."*

Creating is like that too. You can read books, take courses, know all *about* creating, and still not be able to *do* it. "So much that's said about creativity is unhelpful and untrue," says Mike Vance, former Imagineer and Dean of Disney University. "You just aren't going to get more creative following the techniques in most books."[29] Knowing *about* creating doesn't mean that you can create real and lasting results any more than knowing *about* piano playing or skiing means that you can play Mozart's sonatas or tackle double black diamond ski runs.

Too often, people who read about creativity assume that insight leads to success. It rarely does. The road to success always leads through practice. Thinking outside the box is a good way to come up with different ways of doing things. It can be an important part of the creative process, but it's far from the whole thing. Creative *doing* has to follow creative *thinking*. Celia and Al gradually discovered that creating required that they learn a new set of skills and a new way of organizing how they applied those skills.

Specific Skills; Generic Skills

Not everyone agrees that creating is skill-based. Some prefer to see creativity much as people saw literacy several hundred years ago. Back then, literacy was thought to be a special trait, a rare gift, limited to those close to God — i.e., monks and priests. Either you had it, or you didn't. Today, many people think that way about creativity. Others see creativity as a breakthrough to higher levels of consciousness, a kind of epiphany that cleanses the doors of perception and allows your intuition to flow. Still others associate creativity with emotional dysfunction, mental disturbance, and bizarre behaviour. However, creating, like literacy, is an interlinked set of skills that anyone can master. I hope that as we develop these skills — individually and in groups — we will make changes in our lives and world that are as significant as those produced by the spread of literacy over the last 500 years.

Some skeptics, like Harvard's Howard Gardner, agree that creating is skill-based, but argue against the notion of *generic* creativity. "A person isn't creative in general," Gardner says. "You can't just say a person is 'creative.' You have to say he or she is creative in X, whether it's writing, being a teacher, or running an organization. People are creative in something." [30]

Gardner is right, as far as he goes. Creating does involve the mastery of *specific*, craft-related "skills in something." You might be a creative painter, a creative gardener, or a creative parent. However, as well as specific "skills in something," creating also requires mastery of a set of skills that are *generic* to *all* forms of creating. Generic skills are higher order skills (meta-skills some call them) that underlie creators' ability to develop and apply specific skills. If skills like sketching, mixing colours, and washing watercolours are aspects of our *know-how*, generic skills such as initiative, patience, and persistence give us the ability *to know how to know-how.* They enable us to create new skills and to deploy old skills in new ways. They let us learn from our own experience, even our failures.

All creators, for example, envision (if only vaguely) the result they want to create. The capacity to craft clear, compelling visions of desired results is a generic skill. Artists have it, musicians have it, architects have it, even a mother envisioning a special birthday party for her child has it. Vision is an essential skill, not only in the arts, but also in life.

Creators ground their vision in reality by continuously assessing where they are relative to the result they envision. A painter steps back from the canvas to check the effect of his last series of brushstrokes. A singer palms one ear to hear herself in a recording studio. To create what matters, you not only have to have a clear and compelling vision of what you want, you must also have an accurate, objective sense of where you are relative to where you want to be.

The most important generic skill that creators master is the capacity to hold vision and reality in creative tension with each other. Doing so sets up an organizing framework for exploration and experimentation. It also establishes a "field" of creative energy, a container for creativity. Within that field, which organizes actions like a magnetic field organizes iron filings, creators set out action steps that enable them to explore, to experiment with process, and learn from their doing. Working within such a framework enables them to get feedback, make adjustments, try again, and gradually shape the finished result they desire.

In the chapters that follow, we will examine these and other generic creating skills. I will show you how to craft powerful visions of both the simplicity and success you want to create. I will show you how to assess your current reality accurately and objectively. You'll learn how to set up and orchestrate creative tension; how to take effective action; how to learn from mistakes and failure; how to build momentum; and how to finish fully and enjoy the fruits of your labor. We will also examine the structure — the simple yet powerful organizing dynamic of creating — that links these skills into a unified, easy-to-use framework for creating desired results. When mastered and combined with specific expertise in something you care about, these universal creating skills can be used to create almost anything you want. With them, you can integrate simplicity and success to produce simplicity on the other side of complexity.

The Art of Creating

"But," you might ask, "if creators such as artists or writers have mastered all these powerful generic skills as you claim, why aren't all of them living the lives they long for?"

Many artists don't know what they know. The are skilled in their particular medium but they lack the generic skills to transfer those specific skills to the rest of their lives. Much artistic and literary creating is intuitive. It's unconscious competence. Before it can be deliberately applied to other aspects of life, creators have to make themselves conscious of that competence. That's where *generic* creating skills can help. As well as helping you learn what you don't know, they help you recognize what you do know and how to apply it.

When I first started teaching people how to create, I was intimidated by artists who came to my information sessions. Not being in the visual arts, I was afraid that artists would be skeptical about generic creating skills. And they were, at first. But almost all of them inevitably come to the same conclusions that Bev, a painter, did in one of my early sessions. After asking pointed and carefully crafted questions, Bev scrunched up her face, then relaxed and blew out a deep breath. "You know," she said, "I came here prepared to disagree that creating could be taught or learned. But what you describe as the creative process is exactly how I make art. I just never thought about the steps and how they fit together as you have. I don't need to take a course to improve my life. I just have to apply my artistic skills to creating what I want in life."

I couldn't have agreed more. There is an art to creating and, for most of us, it requires new skills and new structures in which to organize those skills. Now, let's turn our attention to the skills and structure with which to create almost anything.

Chapter Seven

The Structure of Creating

*By accurately representing the world of today while stub-
bornly holding out a genuine vision of a better future, we
generate the field of creative energy that is implied in the
famous quote from Goethe:*
　Whatever you can do or dream you can, begin it.
　Boldness has genius, power and magic in it.

Christopher Childs, *The Spirit's Terrain*

At this point, you may be tempted to protest, "But *I'm* not a creator. I've never created anything, let alone what truly matters to me. I don't know how to create."

I beg to differ. I think you *do*. You may not know *how* you do, but at some level and in some ways, you know how to create. Naturally; intuitively. When you make a special sandwich for your child or Sunday brunch for your soul mate, you create. When you pick out clothes for a first date or an important interview, you create. When you host a dinner party for cherished friends, you create. When you complete a project that you care about at work, you create. When you plan, till, and tend a garden, you create.

True, you might not make art, but you *do* create. You focus on results you care about and bring them into being. If your result is an expression of love — your gift to yourself and to the world — then it truly *is* creating. If you do it well enough, it just might become art.

You Are Already A Creator

We intuitively know how to create simple things like sandwiches and birthday parties. When I write a letter to my brother, I follow the same basic steps that all creators use when they create anything. I start with a result I want to achieve. I envision the kind and quality of letter I want to send. A quick and chatty one? Or one in which I share deep feelings? When I'm clear about what I want my letter to look and read like, I assess current reality, my starting point. I take stock of my mood. I sort out my thoughts and feelings so I can convey them clearly. Finally, I draft a letter. I read it over, then revise it until it matches the letter I envisioned. Then I send it.

The description makes the process of creating more linear and straightforward than it often is. Sometimes I'm not sure about the kind of letter I want until I've done a draft and the purpose of the letter reveals itself in the writing. Still, I start with the idea of a letter in mind. I assess current reality. And I take action to produce and send the letter. This is the same process with which Picasso created art, Maya Angelou creates poetry, and Yvonne Chouinard created *Patagonia*, the outdoor clothing company. Although the creations we bring into being may not be as complex and impressive as those of such famous creators, we *too* create.

From Unconscious Incompetence to Flowing Competence

When we craft small creations, we don't think about the process, it flows organically. Letter writing and gourmet sandwich-making are simple for us because we've practiced them for years. We're competent at creating these results but not fully conscious of that competence.

Competence in any skill proceeds through four stages: from unconscious incompetence to conscious incompetence, to conscious competence, and finally, to unconscious competence.

Think about the stages children go through learning to write a letter.

At first, they are *unconsciously incompetent*. They don't know how to write and don't know that they don't know how. They scribble on a piece of paper and hand it to you, saying, "Here Mommy, here's a letter for you." We laugh and praise their effort.

Next comes *conscious incompetence*. Now they know that they don't know how to write. This is a frustrating stage. It requires learning, practice, and mistakes. Ask them to write a letter and they'll likely say, "No, it's too hard. It takes too long. I don't know how." Sound familiar?

As they improve, they move into *conscious competence*. They know how to write and know that they do. They still have to think about it. They may ask you for a little help, but ask them to write to Grandma and they'll do so without difficulty or complaint.

Finally, after years of consciously writing letters, they reach a state of *unconscious competence* wherein they can sit down and dash off a beautiful letter without thinking about it. As I said above, in this state of competence, the process seems to flow organically.

We *are* all creators. However, one reason that we don't see ourselves as creators is that most of us do not recognize our creating skills as skills. We're not conscious of our creative competence. We're not aware of it. Accessing your positive creative core can change that.

Your Positive Creative Core

To underscore your experience and skills as a creator, I'd like you to take a moment to think of creations you have already created, things you cared about enough to bring into being. They can be anything that mattered to you, from a birthday cake for your child to a new *PowerPoint* presentation at work, from a tidy writer's workspace tucked into a corner of your bedroom to a new workshop in your garage. A creation could be a deck, a garden, a dinner party, a committee report, a flower arrangement, a trout fly... anything that you cared enough about to bring into being. Think back over your life and make a list of as many such creations as you can think of. Write them down. Do this before you continue reading. It'll help you with what comes next.

* * * * * * *

Once you've written your list, go over each creation and recall the process of bringing it into being. Remember what it felt like to complete the creation, to have it in your life. Allow yourself to feel a deep sense of appreciation toward each creation and to feel gratitude toward yourself for creating it. Let the reality of these creations fill you with the confidence that you have skills, knowledge, and experience that you may not have been aware that you possessed.

Together, these creations make up your *positive creative core*. They are proof that you know how to create. They're a critical part of your current reality. No matter what you want to create, your creative core provides a solid base from which to start. When you link the energy that arises from this core competence to what you want to create, results you thought impossible become doable. When you're tempted to dismiss yourself as a creator, get in touch with your positive creative core. Take a few moments to appreciate what you've *already* created. You'll be surprised at the power it generates and how good it makes you feel.

Another reason that we don't see ourselves as creators is that we are not aware of the structure — the framework — in which we arrange and apply our skills. Without understanding *how* we create results, we find it difficult to *deliberately* apply our skills to more complex desires such as integrating simplicity and success. When faced with difficult or challenging situations, most of us fall back on what we know best — problem-solving. Then, when problem-solving fails to produce the results we want, we take it as proof that we do not know how to create.

But don't despair. By mastering the skills and framework of creating outlined here, you can develop the conscious competence you need to deliberately create what matters. With practice, that competence will become a natural part of you. Acts of creating will flow effortlessly and organically. You will shift from a reactive problem-focussed stance to a creator's results-focussed stance. You'll be well on your way to creating the simplicity on the other side of complexity.

The Skills and Framework of Creating

Although there is no recipe, no formula for creating, there is, as there is in jazz or the blues, a *form* or *framework* that is common to all acts of creation. This framework includes the generic, higher-order skills and practices that all creators use (consciously or intuitively) to guide their energy, desires, and actions in the direction of what matters. It also includes the way that those skills must be arranged in relation to each other, a specific but powerful structure for creating.

Although there are as many different ways of creating as there are creators, all creators start by accessing the creative tension that arises out of the gap between a vision of a result they want to create and the current reality of that result. They hold that tension gently in their mind. They explore it, play with it, and use it to try out actions, note their results, and try again. Finally, by learning from mistakes and successes, they resolve the tension by shaping their creation so that it matches their vision of it. The list below will give you an overview of the basic creating skills or practices. The diagram will show you how they form a framework that you can use to create almost anything. We'll explore all of these skills and the framework in detail later.

To Set Up Creative Tension:

1. **Know What You Want:** Clarify what matters. Craft a clear, compelling *vision* of your result. Create engaging mental images of that result.

2. **Know What You Have:** Ground yourself in *current reality*. Accurately and objectively assess the current state of the vision; know where you are relative to where you want to be. A good principle to guide your objectivity is *"Describe* reality; don't *judge* it!"

3. **Hold Vision and Reality Together to Set Up** *Creative Tension*: To create *a framework for action* — a field of possibilities — hold vision *and* reality in mind at the same time. Use the tension that emerges out of the gap between vision and reality to take action and produce results. Creative tension provides the energy of creation.

To Work With Creative Tension:

4. **Put First Things First:** *Focus* on what matters most. Create hierarchies of value. *Choose* actions that support your desired result — in spite of circumstances, problems, or adversity. If actions aren't obvious, experiment; make some up and test them against vision.

5. **Start Small and Build Patterns of Success:** Start with *doable steps*. Build competence and confidence through small successes. Then *stretch* for more challenging results.

6. **Trust Your Intuition:** Open to your own deep wisdom. Let the creative spirit flow through you. Let go of the idea of controlling the process. *Be open* to new ideas.

To Resolve Tension Towards final Results:

7. **Craft the Process As You Go:** *Experiment*, seek feedback, learn from experience. Try, test, and try again. *Create and adjust*, create and adjust…. Lay down your path as you go.

8. **Build Momentum to Use When Motivation Falters:** Use all the steps to build *momentum*. This ensures that you can generate results even when motivation fades. Keep moving; keep one eye on your vision, the other on your next steps. *Always have a place to go next*.

9. **Finish Fully**: Follow through, complete your results, then cele-
brate, enjoy the fruits of your labor, and let go. Use the energy of
completion to take on new creations.

Creators integrate these nine skills in a dynamic framework that
generates a tension-charged organizing framework — a container for
creating — as shown in the diagram that follows.

THE FRAMEWORK OF CREATING

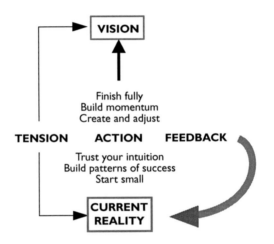

As you work your way through the skills and structure that make up
this framework, you will see that the creative process is a powerful system for organizing and taking actions that support desired results — in
spite of current reality. By embracing the *whole* process — vision, reality,
and action — you will be able to simplify, clarify, and harmonize the
process of producing results. Because the creative process embraces and
transcends problems and complexity as part of current reality, it is more
powerful than problem-solving. It incorporates structural conflict into its
own structure, and it transposes its oscillating structure into a simple,
resolving one.

Above all, as you work with this framework, you will realize that creators practice their craft. You'll see that insight and intellect alone do not
yield desired results. You'll see that the road to both simplicity and success always leads through diligent, daily practice.

The Core Components of Creating

Although all nine skills interact to form the framework out of which creative tension emerges, three components, *vision*, *reality*, and *action* form the basic core. We'll examine all the skills later. Here, I want to give you an overview of the core components and how they interact.

A *Vision* is a clear, compelling mental picture, a description of the result you want to create. It doesn't have to be perfect; some creators' visions are detailed, others' are less so. A vision of an end result only has to be clear enough that you'd recognize that result if you created it.

Current Reality is an objective, accurate description of where you're starting relative to where you want to end up. It includes what already works, what skills, experiences, and resources you already have, and what forces are working on your behalf. It includes your positive creative core. It also includes problems, limitations (real and perceived), adverse circumstances, negative feelings, and other forces that might work against you.

Action Steps include all the strategies and tactics, the steps — large and small — that you take to get you from where you are to where you want to be. In creating, you don't need an elaborate plan or detailed list of steps. When you're secure in the creative framework, you can let go and flow. You can experiment and see what emerges. All you need are vision, current reality, and your next few steps. You make up the rest as you go.

Together, the core elements — vision, current reality, and action steps — form the *structure* of the creative process. Moreover, as with ingredients in a soufflé or parts in a machine, the core components must be arranged — connected to each other — in a particular way.

When *Current Reality* Drives the Action

If you start creating focussed on current reality, you're likely to set up a problem-focussed, intensity-driven framework, as Celia and Al did when they first simplified. They saw the reality of their fast paced lives as a problem and simplicity as the solution. When reality drives the action, circumstances, not vision, become the predominant motivating force.

The process unfolds as follows

1. **Current Reality:** What's happening? What are my most pressing problems?
2. **Vision:** Given that reality, where *should* I go? What *should* I create?
3. **Action:** How do I get there?

In this arrangement, problems, limitations, and lack of resources predominate; intensity drives the action. Because they focussed on a stressful reality from which they wanted to escape, Celia and Al did things that they thought they *should* do rather than things they *wanted* to do. Recall that Celia said they "had to" escape the city. When current reality drives the action, goals become reactions. Worse, you limit your goals to what you think you can achieve with what you currently have. You sacrifice vision to the demands of circumstances. If you view simplicity as a solution to the problems and complexity of current reality, your efforts will produce temporary results. If getting rid of clutter is more important than crafting a compelling vision of what truly matters, you'll focus more on clutter than on creating what matters.

When *Vision* Drives the Action

To be effective, the components of the creative dynamic must be arranged as shown below.

In this arrangement, vision drives the action — not current reality or circumstances.

1. **Vision:** Where do I *want* to go? What do I *love*? What do I most *want* to create?
2. **Current Reality**: Where am I? What do I have? What's already in place?
3. **Action:** How do I bridge the gap? What are my next steps?

Although the core components are the same in both examples, the *structure* — the relationship between the elements — is not. In this structure, vision guides your efforts. You stretch for what you most want and accept where you are as your starting point. You use the tension between vision and reality to invent a process for getting from where you are to where you want to be. When Celia and Al learned to craft clear, compelling visions of what they truly wanted to create — independent of the problems, circumstances, and adversity they faced in current reality — creating what they wanted became easier. Problems faded away; their life became simpler, more harmonious, and more successful.

Simplicity seekers who envision the specific creations that they'd love to bring into being — and the higher values and purpose that those creations serve — are more likely to create and sustain both simplicity and success than are those who react or respond to circumstances. You can tell that you have shifted into the creative orientation when "I should" and "I must" changes to a deeply felt "I want" followed by "I choose." The uptight, stressed feeling so common to problem-solving gives way to the flowing, fully engaged feeling of being in the creative process. A big part of "flow" comes from harnessing creative tension.[31]

The Power of Creative Tension

Holding vision and current reality in mind simultaneously sets up a discrepancy, a gap between where you are and where you want to be. Within that gap, a powerful energizing force is created. Creative tension is the engine of the creative process. Stretch a thick rubber band. Feel the tension in it. Feel its tendency to move, to resolve the tension. Similarly, creative tension seeks resolution; it wants to move. Creators use that tendency toward movement to power and guide their actions in the direction of results they want to create.

Close your eyes for a moment and imagine seeing someone you are attracted to across a crowded room. Or imagine that you are out hiking and have a strong desire to see what's beyond the next ridge. Can you feel a slight tightening in your belly, a quickening of your energy, a tendency to move toward what attracts you? That's what creative tension feels like. Anything you *truly* want to create, when held in tension with the reality that you don't yet have it, creates an energizing tension in you.

There are three ways to resolve that creative tension:

1. Give up your vision. Choose in favour of things as they are.
2. Compromise. Lower your standards, and settle for a lesser vision.
3. Take action that consistently moves you toward your vision.

Only the third way *consistently* leads towards desired results.

If you give up or compromise your vision, you reduce or eliminate the gap between vision and reality. There won't be enough tension produced to move you toward the results you want. Circumstances will become the driving force. You're likely to slip back into problem-solving. However, by mastering the skills of the creative framework, you can shift the power in your life away from circumstances and put it squarely in your own hands.

Visionaries *vs.* Realists

Would-be creators sometimes identify with the part of the creative framework that they think is most important, often to the point of taking on a role or persona associated with that part.

Visionaries, for example, often act as if only lofty, far off results matter. They focus primarily on imaginative scenarios of what could be. They can be impatient with the pedestrian concerns of the realist. They would rather spin out visions than act. Without the visionary in our self and our groups, we can't stretch for what most matters. But by themselves visionaries rarely generate results.

Realists, on the other hand, have their feet planted firmly on the ground, or on the bottom line. They argue that only realistic, doable goals are important. They focus primarily on current reality, and on what is reasonable given current skills and resources. They're not interested in pie-in-the-sky visions. However, without realists, the vision is not grounded in reality. We don't know where we actually are. Again, results become difficult to generate.

Finally, *activists* quickly become impatient with both visionaries and realists, especially when they argue with each other or get locked into endless discussions about vision *vs.* reality. Activists just want to do something — anything! The credo of one energetic activist I coached was "Pitter patter, let's get at 'er. Let's just *do something!*" However, without the guidance of the creative framework, action degenerates into reaction.

Although there are obvious strengths in each approach, there are dangers in over-relying on any *one* of them. I'm reminded of the Buddha's story about three blind sages arguing about an elephant. One sage feels the trunk and claims the elephant is snake-like. Another feels a leg and says the elephant is like a tree. The third sage rubs the body and declares an elephant to be like a strong wall. Because they focus only on a part, none of the sages is able to comprehend the elegant, integrated whole that is the elephant. None is able to access the simple elegant power that comes from comprehending the place of the part within the whole. I'm afraid that many of our modern self-help sages often make the same mistake.

Role Conflict in Teams

Much of the conflict and complexity I see in couples, families, and organizations results from a failure to see the whole elephant. Instead, individuals struggle with each other to prove the superiority of the role they identify with. I worked, for example, with a fast-growing financial services company in which the *realist* Chief Financial Officer refused to listen to the *visionary* President's lofty ideas for a simpler, more socially and environmentally responsible approach to investing. She thought it would bankrupt the company. As a major investor and key executive, the CFO saw her role as keeping the company focussed on a realistic, achievable bottom line. However, her opposition to anything "visionary" caused most executive meetings to deteriorate into unpleasant stand-offs between her and the president. That conflict not only prevented the changes envisioned by the president, it also got in the way of existing business operations.

In the absence of a mutually agreed upon vision, the hard-charging sales manager felt it was his *activist* duty to "get at 'er" and make money in whatever way he could. He led his troop of sales agents off on tangents that had more to do with quick returns and high commissions than either the President's vision or the CFO's bottom line. He reminded me of the World War II pilot who radioed in from somewhere over the Pacific to say, "I'm lost, but I'm making good time!" The company stalled. Morale and productivity eroded. Rather than moving toward desired results, employees spent precious time, energy, and resources fighting among themselves and reacting to crises. The result was organizational dysfunction and a reduced bottom line.

It wasn't until I conducted a three-day *Strategic Design* retreat for the executive team that all team members fully grasped that vision, current reality, and action formed a framework for producing outstanding results. At the end of the retreat, as the group was sipping cold beer on the deck of the rustic retreat center, the CFO turned to the President and said, "Okay, Dave, I get it. Vision, reality, *and* action. We need them all." She smiled and then said, "I believe I'm ready to listen to that vision of yours now."

Dave broke into a grin that lit up the afternoon. He put down his beer so he could talk with both hands and then launched into an animated description of the future he envisioned. His impromptu speech and the CFO's newfound support marked a turning point in the company's road to both social and financial success. Even the activist sales manager fell into line and began making money in a way that served the higher social and environmental vision.

Role Conflict in Relationships

I've seen the same role-playing dynamics at play in relationships. Celia, for example, was more visionary than Al. He, in turn, felt that he had to ground what he called Celia's "over-the-top" visions in his "down-to-earth" version of reality. Couples in the throes of relationship difficulties often over-identify with one of the key creating skills. "I'd like to go back to school and study...." says the *Visionary*. The *Realist* reacts with, "That's crazy. We can't afford it. It's not realistic." And the fight is on.

When couples rigidly adopt one of the creating skills, they often see their partner's stance as a problem. They try to solve it by pushing it away, blocking it, or just ignoring it, hoping it will go away by itself. Instead, the conflict intensifies. During coaching, I help each partner integrate all three of the core components into their own creating approach. Each needs to be Visionary *and* Realist to set up the creative framework and generate creative tension. Each needs Activist skills to harness the tension, put ideas into action, and learn from experience. Working together the couple can integrate these roles into a shared framework for *co-creating* what matters to them both. They'll still be able to pursue individual interests without affecting relationship harmony. In fact, that harmony will probably increase.

Sabotaging Your Self

It's not just in group situations that over-identifying with a creating skill causes ineffectiveness and conflict. By over-identifying with the role of visionary, realist, or activist, individuals, too, can limit their capacity to create. I often see dreamy *visionaries* with great ideas for simplifying their lives and becoming successful but who lack a solid grounding in reality and a well-developed capacity for action. I see up-tight *realists* focussed only on the bottom line, with no vision, limited action, and way too much reaction. I see *activists* who, like the sales manager above, feel like they're making good time but have no idea where they're headed. Often that direction is merely away from what they don't want.

Most of us are a bit like the three blind sages. Sometimes we focus on vision; other times we focus on problems. In crisis, we react. However, using just one of the core skills takes too much energy. Because we have to force results, we quickly run out of steam. We end up where we started, only more frustrated. Focussing on one element rarely produces the results we truly want. Integrating all three core skills into our behaviour and working within the creative framework can make a huge difference in our effectiveness.

Take a moment and reflect on your own approach. Do you see yourself in one of these roles? Do you act as a Visionary? Or a Realist? Or an

Activist? Is it always one role in particular? Or do you take on different roles in different settings and contexts?

What about your partner? Does he or she identify with one of these roles? Which one? Is there ever conflict between you because, locked into these roles, you cannot see the whole picture? If so, think about what you might do to see the bigger picture — the whole elephant.

The Creative Framework as A Map

The creative framework can serve as a map for crafting simplicity and success. Using it, you can steer by a clear vision of what you want. You can orient yourself by objectively observing current reality. You can set a strategic course for action by choosing the path of least resistance between where you are and where you want to end up.

You can use the map to plan. You can use it to order and guide your actions. You can use it to evaluate results in relation to vision and make adjustments based on feedback. The map can help you learn from your experience (including mistakes and failure). It can keep you focussed as you craft the results that matter to you — regardless of circumstances, setbacks, or problems.

By developing a capacity to create, you can transcend circumstances. You can integrate simplicity and success. You can embrace the complexity of everyday life and move through its messiness to the simplicity on the other side of complexity. Using the framework as a map and applying the creating skills to your everyday life, you can consistently produce the results you long for in life, work, relationships… in whatever matters to you. As you read the following description of the way one woman used the creative framework as a map for creating the life she longed for, keep in mind the skills and structure that make up that framework.

Putting It All Together: Sarah's Story

When I first met her, Sarah had been recently widowed. She'd quit her job in the city and moved to the island where I live. She came to one of my workshops looking to rebuild her life. During the workshop she listed a number of small, concrete results she wanted to produce, including a writing space, a brochure for her consulting service, and a circle of friends to connect with. When pushed to stretch for what most mattered to her, she outlined detailed criteria for a long-term vision of what she wistfully called her "dream cottage."

Although she confessed that she didn't really believe she'd ever achieve it, she told us that she longed to live in a cozy, post-and-beam cottage by the edge of the sea. As she thought about her vision of that cottage, she realized she'd like it to have at least a thirty mile view, to be situated on a roomy, beach-front parcel of land with space for a garden in which she could grow her own organic food. The site had to be rural, yet close to a well-treed, small town with ample cultural amenities such as a library, bookstores, coffee shops, good restaurants, and a thriving arts community. Other essential design criteria were a desire to spend no more than $50,000 and to be able to easily add a studio, solarium, and extra bedrooms to the cottage over time.

Participants in the workshop were impressed with Sarah's ability to visualize the results she wanted. However, all of them thought her vision was "unrealistic." No one thought she'd ever create such a spectacular sounding result on such a modest budget. I pointed out the judgmental nature of their comments and urged Sarah to keep her vision bright and clear, and to simply observe reality as objectively as she could. With my encouragement, Sarah went ahead with work on her dream cottage project in spite of her own and others' doubts.

"I did it," she said, "more to learn about the skills and form of creating than with any real hope of actually producing the final result." In her vision, she didn't see herself even getting close to achieving it for at least ten years. "I did not, myself, believe it was possible," she confessed to me in her delightful French-Canadian accent. "But, hey, I thought to myself, what do I have to lose? Nothing. And lots, I thought, to learn."

Sarah's first step was to clarify her *vision*. To the above design criteria, she added other specifics such as the hours of sunlight her house would receive, average temperature and rainfall levels, and proximity to urban centers with large French-speaking populations to support her translation and consulting work. She included an intangible sense of "comfort," a sense of belonging in that place, of being deeply at home in her little cottage and its surroundings. She also envisioned herself becoming a well-regarded member of the local community and creating a thriving, meaningful translation business.

As she added detail to her vision and practiced visualizing her desired result as if it were fully completed, she said it got "brighter, more exciting" and took on a life of its own. "It was so compelling," she said. "It had a pull I could not resist."

Sarah found it difficult, at first, not to let herself be overwhelmed by the brilliance of her newly crafted vision. However, she faithfully followed the workshop process and grounded that vision in a careful, objective assessment of *current reality*.

The most obvious aspect of her reality was a lack of funds. She was almost broke and lived in an area in which waterfront property started at $500,000. She liked the island, but noted that as well as the cost of real estate, it failed to live up to some of the key criteria she'd outlined in her vision. "Winters are too wet, too grey, and too long," she said. "There is no French population nearby. My village is nice, but it has none of the cultural institutions or activities I desire. I can't afford a car to travel to the larger town, so I often feel trapped."

In spite of the gap between her vision and current reality, Sarah practiced holding both in mind simultaneously for fifteen minutes each morning and evening. She used the creative framework and its dynamic tension to energize and guide her actions. She began to take small *action steps* toward making her vision a reality.

She researched other parts of the country based on the criteria she'd specified. She told me later that she hadn't thought of research as an action step, but quickly discovered it was an essential one. Using the telephone, Internet, and government information offices, she gained valuable new information, particularly about weather patterns and housing prices. Much of what she found out didn't help her. She made mistakes, fixed them, and carried on. She eventually narrowed her search down to the western province of Saskatchewan and the Atlantic province of New Brunswick.

"I dropped all the Saskatchewan sites pretty quick," she said, "Although they get good sun, it can go down to 40 degrees below zero — in Fahrenheit *and* Celsius! That's too cold for me."

That left New Brunswick. Sarah focussed her efforts more tightly and zeroed in on several small towns in that maritime province just above Maine. She researched each town in depth. She was excited by what she discovered and felt her enthusiasm for the project growing. "Houses there cost one-fifth to one-tenth what they cost here," she said. "I have to go there; I want very much to see those towns."

Although she had no cash on hand when she began, halfway through the six-week workshop Sarah received a severance cheque of $6,000 from her previous employer. A bank teller suggested she put it in an RRSP[32] and borrow an additional $6,000 against it for that year's contribution. Sarah took that suggestion and felt her confidence and momentum increase as she realized she now had, by her standards, a sizable stake of seed-money.

Several months into her project, Sarah used the frequent flyer points she and her late husband had accumulated to fly to New Brunswick. There she fell in love with one of the towns she'd discovered in her research. "It met all my criteria," she told me. "It even had," she marveled, "two restaurants listed in the gourmet book *Where To Eat In Canada!*"

Although she was unable to find suitable property listed in the local real estate offices, she was convinced she would live near that town and refused to return home until she found the place she wanted. She searched the countryside for unlisted properties. One afternoon she spotted a piece of land that met all of her criteria.

"It was perfect," she said, "Open to the sea, a spectacular site for a house, surrounded by colorful meadows of wildflowers and backed by a small, sweet smelling forest. Only one small problem. It was not for sale."

Undaunted, determined to make her vision a reality, Sarah tracked down the landowner. She shared her vision with him and persuaded him to sell her ten acres. She purchased the lot with a loan backed by her RRSP. Before she left the area she made contact with a young designer/builder who had been searching for an opportunity to build an ecologically designed, solar-heated, post-and-beam cottage to showcase his talent and ideas as an eco-designer. He agreed to design and build Sarah a simple, modular cottage for far less than a regular contractor would charge if she would give him free rein to design the structure he wanted to build.

"He showed me several examples of what he had in mind," said Sarah. "They looked fine to me. So I said 'Okay' and we shook hands and made a deal." She leveraged another loan from a local bank using the builder and landowner as references and the new land as collateral and had the builder drawing up plans and ordering building materials before she left for the airport.

When I last saw her, Sarah was in our local post office mailing twenty bulky, heavily taped cardboard boxes to her new address in New Brunswick. While we spoke, tears ran down both our faces. "This was my greatest dream," she told me, "my vision. Myself, I did not think it was possible, but I was so excited. I loved the idea of that house by the sea. I could feel the tension, the pull to make it happen. I could not stop myself from working on it even though so many said it was impossible. And, now, next month, I move in."

The whole thing, her land, her house, her garden, cost her under $50,000. Not bad for just six months! As I turned to leave the post office, Sarah grabbed my sleeve. With a grin on her face as wide as the ocean view she'd just bought, she said, "As soon as I get there, I'm gonna start creating myself a nice little car." I had no doubt she'd succeed.

Sarah's story exemplifies the power that can arise out of the bold action Goethe recommends in the couplet that led off this chapter. It shows how boldness can be focussed and guided by the creative framework and sustained by the energy of creative tension.

I must tell you, however, that the time frame is not typical. Few clients work as hard or produce the results Sarah did in such a short time. It usually takes as long to get good at creating as it does to get good at any other complex set of skills, such as skiing, cello playing or public speaking. It takes the same dedicated practice. Most folks take from nine months to two years to accomplish the kinds of results Sarah did. I tell Sarah's story, however, to show how, by mastering the form and practice of creating, anyone can integrate simplicity and success. By crafting a clear, compelling vision, grounding that vision in reality, and taking action, step by step, you too can transcend complexity and make the complicated simple. With practice, you might find yourself living out your own dreams with the same kind of boldness that Sarah lived hers — and discovering for yourself the genius, power, and magic that come from mastering your own creative process. Along the way, I hope that you too will learn to craft the life you long for, a life that gracefully integrates simplicity and success.

The place to start crafting that life is envisioning what you most want to create.

Chapter Eight

Driven By Vision

Vision has power, for through vision you can easily reach beyond the ordinary to the extraordinary. Vision can help you organize your actions, focus your values, and see clearly what is relevant in current reality.

Robert Fritz, *The Path of Least Resistance*

The place to start *creating* is at the *end*, with a clear, compelling vision of a result you want to create. That's what Sarah did. Her thoughtful, well-crafted vision of a "dream cottage" generated so much power that she felt pulled along by it. However, for many, knowing what you want is not as easy as it was for Louise. "Learning what to want," said Sir Geoffrey Vickers, author of *Freedom in a Rocking Boat*, "is the most radical, the most painful, and the most creative act in life." [33]

Crafting clear, compelling visions of what matters can be so painful that many of us never do it. Is it any wonder that we go through life doing what is second, third, or tenth most important to us, reacting and responding to the problems and circumstances that assault us?

Part of the difficulty stems from confusion around the word "vision." It is often used interchangeably with words like "purpose," "mission," or "goal." Although there are similarities between these terms, it is important to sort out their specific meanings for yourself. Here's how the *Concise Oxford Dictionary* defines them:

Purpose: an object to be attained, a thing intended.

Mission: a particular task or goal assigned to a person or a group.

Goal: the object of a person's ambition or effort, a destination, an aim.

Vision: a thing or idea perceived vividly in the imagination.

Imagine a couple who is interested in simple living, ecological responsibility, and creating a successful business. "Our *purpose*," they say, "is to create a simple yet rich life in harmony with the systems that sustain all life, and to help others do the same." They add that, "Our *mission* is to make simple, affordable, eco-friendly housing available to everyone in our bioregion." And "Our primary *goals* are to design and build our own eco-friendly home, develop a business to help others do the same, write a book, and offer workshops on eco-friendly housing."

Purpose answers the question "why?" Mission specifies the strategy or "way" this couple chooses to live their purpose. Goal refers to specific "hows," to the actions and results that will mark their progress toward completing their mission and realizing their purpose. All three words describe *results* that the couple wants to produce — the "whats" of "what matters?" These results form a hierarchy of values and desires that ranges from big to little, primary to secondary, and from things they want for their own sake to things that support more important results.

Vision can be applied to purpose, mission, and goals. Vision asks the question, "What would it look like if I successfully produced the result I want? What would it look like if I achieved my purpose? If I succeeded at my mission? If I achieved my specific goals? What would it look like if I created what I *most* want to create?

A vision is a clear mental picture of a result that you want to create. It's a compelling image, an idea perceived vividly in your imagination. Shaped into a vision, results become more doable. A clear, compelling vision of a desired result generates energy. It inspires you to greater effort. It helps you see where you are relative to where you want to be. But remember, it's not *just* vision that generates power. It's the creative tension that arises out of the gap between vision and reality that generates the energy of creating. To set up creative tension, start by crafting a clear, compelling vision of the results you want.

Getting Started: An Example

Three questions can help you clarify a vision of what you want to create. They are:
- What result do I want to create?
- Why do I want it?
- What would it look like if I successfully created that result?

Try this yourself. Take a moment now and choose a simple, tangible result that you want to create. Write that result at the top of a sheet of paper. Below it, write two short paragraphs. In the first, list the reasons why you want to create this result. This will help you discover whether this is a creation that you want for its own sake, or something that supports a more important result. It will help you decide if this is something that matters or just a passing fancy.

In the second paragraph, describe what the desired result would look like if you created it. How big is it? What colour is it? What features does it have? What makes it unique? If the result is something non-physical, such as a job or a relationship, describe the aspects and qualities that make it what you want. Describe the result as if you had completed it.

Here's an example of how a friend of Al's (an engineer) answered these questions for a specific result he wanted to create as follow-up to the workshop he took with Celia and Al:

- **What do I want?** *A high quality, handcrafted mountain bike made from recycled parts.*
- **Why do I want it?** *I want the challenge of building a great bike cheaply. I want to get in shape and be healthy. I want to live simply, drive less, and create less pollution. I want to spend time outdoors, not money on gas. I want to have fun exploring the trails up behind my house with my friends.*
- **What would it look like if I successfully created that result?** *The bike is a silver-grey, dual-suspension, aluminum-framed bike with carbon forks, grip shifters, top of the line Shimano drivetrain, and an independently suspended crank. It weighs 25 pounds and cost less than $500. I love riding it and feel proud that I made it myself.*

A vision acts as an attractor, a beacon. It draws you forward. When held in tension with current reality, it generates the energy needed to organize decisions and action in support of what matters. It provides a clear picture and a set of criteria against which to measure your progress and eventual success. Always use "vision" as the short form of "a vision of a desired end result." A vision is not a thing in itself. It is not an affirmation that you put out to the universe and passively expect to receive results in return. It's a clear, compelling description of a result that you care for enough to choose to *create*.

Vision is a unifying force. It's an overarching organizing principle like the long line or theme of a piece of music. The things you create will be variations on the themes that make up the music of your life. A clear, compelling vision helps you focus your values and organize your actions. It helps you change heaps of pieces and parts into satisfying wholes. Some visions, such as a vision of your life, a business, or a career will be large and all encompassing. Others, such as a vision of a cottage by water, or a book you want to write, will be smaller. Some, such as a deck on a cottage, an organic garden, or a birthday party for your child, will be smaller yet. You need a vision for each result that you want to create.

A vision is also an impelling force. It motivates and empowers you. It helps you persevere in the face of difficult circumstances and adversity. It enables you to stretch beyond limits and to produce extraordinary results. Over time, the results you create will naturally and organically accumulate into the life you envisioned so vividly in your mind. The rest of your life, as Sarah's life did, could turn on a vision you craft today, tomorrow, or over the next few weeks.

After he built his mountain bike, Richard the bike builder radically simplified his life. His success prompted him to build more bikes, which he sold to friends. Emboldened by that further success, he quit his engineering job, downsized to a smaller house, opened a shop, and began living a simple, yet rich, and fully engaged life as a custom bike builder. "I'm happy now," he says. "Happier by far than when I was engineering with a large firm and never had time to get out on the trails with my friends. Now people pay me to take them out riding. It's wonderful."

10 Practices For Crafting Clear, Compelling Visions

These guidelines — call them skills or practices — will help you clarify what you want. Following them will ensure that you craft clear and compelling visions for the results you want.

1. Go For What Matters *Most* to You

Sandra was a client of mine who had trouble getting to the things that mattered because she felt she had to clear her to-do list first. She spent all day worrying about the things on that list and had no energy left to do what mattered. When I asked her to dedicate at least one hour to creating what mattered before she tackled her to-do list, she discovered she had energy to burn. If you focus on what matters most, that same kind of creative energy can be yours.

The first step is to shift your focus from what you *don't* want to what you *do* want. You're not likely to create health if you're focussed on disease. You're not likely to create elegant simplicity if you're focussed on the stress and problems of your current life. You're not likely to create the future you most want if you're focussed on the past and trying to fix it. Or yourself. If you find yourself still slipping into a problem-focussed stance, shift your focus by asking, "If I could have whatever I *most* deeply desire, what would it be?"

Imagine that what you want *is* possible and that money, talent, experience, and failure are not issues. *What would you want?* Ask yourself the following variations. Try to answer from the perspective of both simplicity and success. Notice if there are discrepancies between a simple home or job and a successful home or job. If so, dig deeper; try to imagine a simple *and* successful home and job. Take a moment and work with these questions now.

- What would my home and neighborhood look like?
- What would my family look like?
- What kind of relationships would I have with friends and colleagues?
- What kind of work would I do? What would success look like?
- What would my finances look like?
- How would I spend my leisure time?
- How would I approach my own learning and growth?
- What would my spiritual life look like?
- What major accomplishments could I look back on and be proud of?

Make notes about each area and any other areas that occur to you. I have clients cluster their ideas by taking a large sheet of paper and drawing a circle in the middle in which they write "A Vision for My Life." Then they draw short lines radiating out from the circle, which connect to smaller circles enclosing each of the above categories. Then, from the smaller circles they draw short lines and more circles that enclose descriptors of each of the specified categories. Once they have finished their notes or cluster describing their life vision, I ask them to make a list of specific creations that they want to create. Then I have them use the three questions that the bike-building engineer used to draft a vision for each creation.

2. Dig Deep to Uncover Your True Desires

Sometimes what we *think* we want is not what we truly want. True vision arises out of deep, heartfelt desire. "The word *desire*," says creativity expert, Stephen Nachmanovitch in *Free Play*, "comes from *desidere*, 'away from your star.' It means elongation from the source, and the concomitant, powerful magnetic pull to get back to the source." Sometimes you have to dig down through layers of ideals and the dust of old desires to get at those sources.

Take Murray. He signed up for one of my long workshops because he hated his job and hoped to create a new career. On the first night of the course, I asked participants to draw up a list of ten things they wanted to create over the next five weeks to ten years. I asked them to pick one result that they wanted to create during the five weeks of the course as a practice project. However, when Murray came to the second session, a week later, he was frustrated. He'd discovered that he didn't want any of the things on his list, or the practice creation he'd chosen. They were all, he told us, things that he thought would make his wife or his parents happy.

I asked him to draw up a new list.

When he returned for the third session, Murray again reported that the results he'd listed were not things he truly wanted. This time he'd made a list of ideals, things that he thought a man his age with a family was "supposed" to want if he were to appear mature, responsible, and successful. Murray was frustrated and anxious about his failure to clarify what he wanted. I asked him to do the visualization in which he imagined that anything he wanted was possible, and that money, skills, education, outside approval, and success could all be assumed. I asked him to imagine what he would want to create under such optimum circumstances.

"I'd make up games," he said, with a sheepish look on his face. "Board games."

"Great," I said. "Is that something you'd truly like to do?"

"Yes," he said, "but..."

"But, what?" I asked.

He seemed nervous, tentative, like a frightened child. "Is it okay to want something like that?" he asked. "I mean, it's kind of a kids' thing, isn't it? What would people think?"

"What people? Okay with who?" I asked. "If it's what you want, it's what you want. It's important to acknowledge that. Just because you want something doesn't mean that you have to act on it; you always have a choice. It is, however, important to know what you *do* want." Murray nodded. "Besides," I added, "do you think the inventors of *Monopoly* or *Trivial Pursuit*s care about what people think?" He grinned.

During the rest of the course, Murray practiced creating by inventing a prototype board game, which we played on the last night. He also got in touch with other deeply held desires. The desire to brew high quality beer from scratch using organic ingredients led him to envision and start a U-Brew business, which he built into a success then sold. Then he started a microbrewery, which he envisions as a "zero-emissions" operation; all wastes will be re-cycled or turned into marketable organic products like exotic mushrooms and pond-raised catfish. Although starting these businesses was stressful, Murray is happier now that he is focussed on what matters to him, now that his path has heart. "It isn't always easy," he told me recently, "but it *is* what I want to do. And that's a lot better than trying to live up to other people's expectations or "shoulding" on myself." I agreed.

3. Don't *Should* On Yourself

Murray had focussed on "ideals," on what he thought he *should* or *ought to* want, not on what he truly did want. Ideals are demands, not desires. They are expectations that we impose on ourselves (and, sometimes, on others) not deeply desired results that we want to bring into being.

Some ideals come from outside, from parents, peers, teachers, authorities, the culture, advertising, and other external sources. From the time we are infants, people tell us what we *should* do. "Go to this school! Dress this way! Buy this car! Find a nice girl! Marry a rich man!" Other ideals come from within. We form them to compensate for underlying beliefs that there is something lacking in us or something wrong that we must fix. "I am bad; therefore, I *should* be good. I am not pretty; therefore, I *should* be pretty. I am stupid; therefore, I *should* be smart. I am not creative, therefore I *should* be creative."

My own most challenging ideal comes from the belief that I am ordinary, and that ordinary is not good enough. To compensate, I tell myself that I *should* be great. This ideal can motivate me initially, but it also causes me to act like an arrogant big shot rather than an ordinary man trying to create what he loves. I spent several years becoming a high paid corporate consultant, not because I loved it but because I thought that I should play in "the bigs." I wanted to measure myself against the best (highest paid) in the most challenging and highly visible arena (the corporate world). I wanted to prove to myself (and others) that *I was* extraordinary.

However, no one is extraordinary. We may *act* extraordinarily, we may *do* extraordinary things, we may *create* extraordinary results, but we are all in our own ways ordinary. Each of us is but one of six billion people on the planet. Furthermore, as the old Zen saying affirms, "One hundred years from now, all new people!" Trying to prove that I *was* great conflicted with my everyday reality, which included ample evidence that I *was not*. Before I could figure out what mattered to me, I had to learn the difference between creating great results and trying to *be* great to compensate for being ordinary. I shifted my focus to doing what mattered. I stopped "shoulding" on myself and focussed on creating the simplicity and success that I longed for. Ironically, in doing so, I learned that my ordinary self was good enough.

You can experience the difference between imposing an ideal on yourself and envisioning and choosing a result you want by doing this short exercise. Think of something that you want in your life. Imagine it as fully completed. Then say to yourself, "I *should* have this. I *must* have it." Then note how you feel. Do you feel heavy, uptight, as if you're carrying a weight that is too heavy for you, or as if you're pushing against the forces in play? That's how I used to feel. That's what it feels like when you impose an ideal on yourself, when, as psychologist Albert Ellis likes to say, you "should" on yourself. "Shoulding" on ourselves, says Ellis, is one of the prime causes of stress, depression, and anxiety.

Now, once again, imagine what you want in your life. As you imagine the result, fully completed, ask yourself, "Do I truly want this result in my life?" If the answer is "Yes," then say, "I choose (the result)," and then note how you feel. Do you feel lighter, more energized, as if you have more power? Do you feel pulled toward the result more than pushed by the demand of the ideal? "Shoulding" on yourself disempowers you. It puts you at odds with reality. *Choosing* a result that you want sets up the "magnetic pull" of creative tension.

In which stance do you choose to live and act?

4. From Concept to Vision

Many of my clients *do* have a sense of what they want. However, their vision is so vague that it lacks the power to motivate them. The results they want are fuzzy generalities such as "success," or "a simple life." It is fine to want such things. However, framed as such, they are not easy to create. General goals such as "success," "a good relationship," and "a simple life" are not visions; they are *concepts*. They won't spur you to action, guide you toward results, or keep you going when the going gets difficult. They are not clear enough that you would recognize them if you created them. They are, however, a good place to start.

Creators use concepts to work out the details of their visions. They play with concepts, try them on, substitute one for another, and experiment in their mind. Through playful exploration, they teach themselves which visions they prefer, which results they want to create.

Concepts are general; vision is specific. To be effective, a concept is best focussed into a clear, specifically articulated vision of a completed result. There's a big difference, for example, between the concept "a nice house" and a vision of a "1500 square foot, three-bedroom, cedar-walled, post-and-beam cottage, with an attached studio, a wood-fired hot-tub on a wrap-around deck, overlooking a quiet sun-lit bay." Which has more power, the concept or the vision?

Because concepts don't give you a clear image of a final result, it is difficult to tell when you have succeeded. Take "financial security" as an example. Within this concept, there is an infinity of possibilities, some that you may want, others that you may not. Those who adopt Joe Dominguez and Vickie Robin's approach to Financial Independence[34] might successfully achieve a vision of "financial security" on $10,000 to $20,000 a year from interest on safe, interest-generating investments combined with a frugal life-style. On the other hand, I've worked with stock brokers who, although they made six figure salaries, struggled to maintain an *image* of financial success that moved further away as other brokers raised the bar of what constituted success. None of those brokers felt that they had created "financial security."

To successfully create what you want, you have to crystallize vague, fuzzy concepts into clear, compelling *visions* of the specific results that you want to create. You have to focus.

5. The Power of Focus

A vision doesn't have to be perfectly clear, just clear enough that you would recognize the result if you created it. Moreover, it doesn't have to be just a mental picture that you hold in your mind. As well as writing out a detailed description of your vision, you can make a drawing, a mind-map, a collage, or even a model of your result. All these devices will give your vision more presence and power. The more focussed your vision is, the more energy it generates. The less focussed it is, the less energy it generates and the less likely you will be to actually create it.

I had a woman in a workshop, for example, who said her vision was "to travel."

"Travel where, Pat?" I asked.

"Everywhere!" she said. The class groaned but I'd seen this before. In fact, every teacher of creating that I've talked with has had at least one student that wanted to "travel everywhere."

"I hear that you want to go everywhere," I said, "but where would you like to go *first*."

"Everywhere!" she said.

I paused, then asked, "Have you done much traveling to date?"

"No," she said, "I just mainly dream about it."

All of us, including Pat, laughed.

"Well," I said, "unless you can specify some place to which you'd like to travel, you're not likely to do much more than dream."

"But," Pat pleaded, "I really do want to travel everywhere."

"Fine," I said, "but 'everywhere' is not a place. It's a concept. It's not somewhere you can actually go in a car or a plane. You can't buy a ticket for it. On your way to everywhere, is there any specific place you'd like to go first?"

"Well," said Pat, "I'd really like to see the island of Kauai in Hawaii."

I suggested that she craft a vision of "A Trip to Kauai" that described the kind and quality of experience that she would love to create, and see what happened. She agreed to do so. A year after the workshop, Pat told me that she'd not only gone to Kauai, but to Thailand as well. She said she still wanted to "travel everywhere," but that focussing her desire into a prioritized list of the most important places she wanted to visit had given her far more power than her fuzzy concept of "everywhere."

Occasionally, clients resist focussing concepts into specific visions. They fear that it would limit them, restrict their freedom and spontaneity. Paradoxically, though, creators find that limits increase power and freedom. "Limits make things visible," says Eric Booth in *The Everyday Work of Art*. "To artists, limitations are not liabilities, they are opportunities to find fresh inventive solutions, to clarify key questions, to prioritize and go deeper."[35]

Although a clearly specified vision does limit you to the result that you choose to create, focussing on that result greatly increases your chances of actually producing it. "Limits yield intensity," adds Stephen Nachmanovitch in *Free Play*. "Form well used can become the very vehicle of freedom." In her early years, when she sang harmony with country rock legend Gram Parsons, folk singer Emmy Lou Harris discovered the freedom inherent in limits. Harris told Parsons' biographer Ben Tong Forres that she had relished "the freedom of being restricted" to singing tenor. She said that she'd grown as a musician and as a person when she'd been forced to sing only the tenor parts.[36]

Crystallizing concepts into clear, compelling visions does limit you in some ways, but those limits also generate the power to create results. "Structure ignites spontaneity," says Nachmanovitch. Moving from concept to vision is a critical step in the creative process.

6. Clarify the Criteria for Success

Crystallizing concepts into visions means specifying the details of the result you want to create. It involves outlining criteria for completion. For example, before he came to me, Ron struggled with the fuzzy concept "An ecological life." He'd tried recycling, cut back on consumption, and tried to eat organic food. However, his job as a technology consult-ant required that he travel extensively and maintain an image of mate-rial success. In coaching, he told me that he was "floundering." I saw that he was shifting back and forth between his concept of an ecological life and his ideal of what a successful professional should look like.

During my workshops and retreats, I suggest that participants ask these kinds of questions:

- *What kind of work do I love doing?*
- *With what kinds of people?*
- *Where would I like to do it?*
- *What would make that work satisfying and fulfilling?*
- *How will I know I'm successful at it?*
- *How much money do I need to make to live comfortably?*
- *What would success look like for me?*
- *What would success feel like — in all ways, not just financial success?*

Using these questions, Ron focussed his concept into this vision: *"Living in an ecologically-designed, solar-heated cottage in the Gulf Islands on an income of about $20,000 a year from website design via the Net; growing my own organic vegetables; trading design work for staples; and joyfully working with community groups to promote ecologically sustainable development."*

This vision had a huge impact on Ron's life. Over time (and by hold-ing it in tension with current reality) he refined it further, eventually choosing the east side of Vancouver Island as a more suitable site for its unfolding. He lives there now, in a rented cabin not unlike the one he envisioned. "I'm not quite there yet," he told me, "but hey, every day I work on making that vision a reality. One day, reality is going to look just like I envision it."

7. Separate what you want from what you believe is possible.

To create what you want, you must believe that what you want is important. However, you do *not* have to believe that it is possible. A vision is a description of what you *truly* want. It does not have to be real-istic. In fact, the more visionary it is, the more power it will have. The place for realistic thinking is in current reality and action, *not* vision. Sarah's story about creating her dream cottage showed that, although a person might not believe their dream is possible, a clear, detailed vision of that dream can be so compelling it moves them to action — and that such action might just pay off, as it did for her.

You want what you want, whether or not it is possible. Indeed, you don't really know whether something is possible or not until you create it. Therefore, a critical step in forming a vision is to separate what you want from what you believe is possible or realistic.

Artists, inventors, scientists, athletes, and other creators work toward visions of results without knowing if they are possible. All they know is that they want the result they envision. Along the way, they set realistic goals and doable action steps for themselves, but the vision itself is not realistic. Only one gold medal is awarded in each Olympic event. Still, knowing that the odds are against them, thousands of athletes vie for spots on their countries' teams. By focussing on their vision and grounding their action in current reality, they strive to create the best performances they can. And one of those performances does win the medal.

One of my first coaching clients was Sharon Wood, the Canadian climber who became the first North American woman to summit Mount Everest. After speeches describing her successful climb and the many hardships she faced (including 100-mph winds, minus 40-degree temperatures, and the difficulties of taking a pee) Sharon is often asked what kept her going. She tells her audience that she had a clear vision of herself standing on the summit and getting down safely. Often a questioner will ask if she always "believed" she'd achieve her vision. "No," she says, "at times it felt impossible. But I knew I wanted it more than I feared that impossibility."

Five years ago, a woman who had been diagnosed HIV positive and was hovering on the edge of full-blown AIDS took one of my workshops. When I saw her recently, she told me that she is healthier than she's been in years and living a full and active life.

"Before that weekend," she said, "I was so afraid of dying and so focussed on fighting the damned disease that I quickly depleted what little energy I had. My 'fighting against' strategy stressed me out and made me more unhealthy. I hadn't even thought about focussing on being healthy because I didn't think it was possible anymore. My criteria for success had dropped to 'just staying alive.' The workshop helped me realize that I really wanted to be healthy — to be fully alive and thriving — whether or not it was possible. I was delighted to realize that I could craft a vision of the kind and quality of health that I most wanted, regardless of my current state of health. Once I did so, I felt energy surge through me. I felt my spirit come back to life. Separating what I wanted from what I thought was possible made all the difference."

So vision does not have to be realistic, or easily achievable. Indeed, it has more power if it involves a stretch toward what *truly* matters to you. Stretch gives the creative framework its tension and its power to generate results.

8. Focus on the end *result*, not the *process* of getting there.

Many people start to craft a vision, then stop themselves with a "Yeah, *but*...!"

"Yeah, I want it, *but* I don't know how to do it." I've done this myself. It's a reflex left over from years of reacting to problems and setting rigid plans. We think we need to know how we're going to create a result before we start creating it. Not so! One of the great things about creating is that you do not have to know *how* you'll create a result before you craft a vision for that result. Process comes later, in "action steps." The "hows" of creating come after you've clarified vision and assessed current reality.

Still, many people confuse end results and processes. When asked what they want some reply, "To win the lottery!" When asked "Why?" they say that, if they had money, then they could have the things they want: "a new car," "security," "leisure time," "a nice home," "freedom," "recognition," "respect," etc. What they *really* want are those things. Winning the lottery is just one way to get them. However, dreaming about a big win, instead actually creating the results you want, is an almost sure way to fail. Focus first on clarifying your vision; leave process for later.

Vision can sometimes arise out of process, out of day-to-day doing. Years ago, before running became the popular activity and big business it is now, I went to Hawaii for a vacation without a pair of sneakers. I hoped to pick up a pair of the canvas Basket Masters I usually wore. However, in the shop, I found a strange assortment of nylon shoes with fancy detailing, raised heels, and waffle-patterned soles. I thought they were merely a strange new fad. Not being trendy, I made disparaging remarks about "high-heeled sneakers" then asked the clerk what the purpose of these strange looking shoes was.

"They're training shoes," he said, "for road running."

Although I regularly pounded out a painful mile per day as part of my "exercise" plan, I didn't know what "road running" was. I told the clerk that I wanted the least fancy shoes he had. He sold me a pair of blue nylon trainers with a white swooshes on the side and a slightly raised heel. On the way back to my hotel, I started jogging. It felt different. My knees didn't hurt. My feet seemed to rebound off the pavement. After a mile, I decided to keep going. Over the next couple of days, I gradually extended my runs until I'd run around Kapiolani Park, a distance of 2.6 miles. Something about that accomplishment flicked the vision switch in my mind. I wanted to see if I could run twice around the park. Suddenly, I had a vision of running five miles. By the end of the vacation, I made that vision a reality, and crafted a new vision of completing the 26-mile Honolulu marathon.

Don't limit your vision to what you already know how to do. Often clients tell me, "I really want to do x but I only have the skill (or money, time, ...) to do y." So they spend their life doing what they *don't* care about, but *do* know how to do. I ask them, "Do you want to create results you care about?" If they say "yes," I ask, "Then why not take the time to develop the necessary skills to create it? Or figure out how to create it with what you have."

It is fine to have a vision of something you don't *yet* know how to create. Creators make up the process as they go. Planning gurus Gary Hammell and G.K. Prahalad urge people not to fit goals and visions to what they believe they are capable of achieving. *Stretch*, not *fit*, they claim is the key to success. They urge us to create "a chasm between ambition and resources." Writing in the March 1993 *Harvard Business Review*, they assert that, "Creating stretch, a misfit between resources and aspirations, is the single most important task." Stretch is another term for creative tension. In other words, create a gap between your vision and current reality, then bridge that gap by learning and creating what you need to make your vision a reality.

Don't worry either about setting your expectations too high. Vision is not an expectation or demand that you impose on yourself. It is simply a description of something you want that does not yet exist. The creating framework allows you to live easily in the gap between vision and reality, without fear, impatience, or anxiety. It provides an organizing structure in which you can see the whole system and where you are in that system. It allows for an almost infinite flexibility in how you create your result. Moreover, it acts as a container for creativity out of which novel and necessary action steps can emerge.

Here's one more hint for separating vision from process: remember that results are things and things are represented by *nouns*; process is action and action is represented by *verbs*. For example, "*Going* to the gym every day" is a process; "going" is the verb. "Strong, well toned muscles" is a result; "muscles" is the noun. Craft your vision using nouns, not verbs. That way you'll focus on *what* not *how*.

9. Include all of what you want in your vision.

Once you have established a result you want, be sure your vision includes *all* aspects of what you want. You can do this by asking yourself, "Would I take it if I could have it?" If the answer is "yes," you obviously want it. If the answer is "no," perhaps there's more to the vision that you haven't yet uncovered. Or maybe the result is just a passing fancy. In one of my workshops, a woman told us that she desperately wanted to be more expressive. She said she was a good listener, but rarely got to tell her own story. So she crafted a vision of what being expressive would look like. However, when I asked her if she'd take it if she got it, she said, "No."

The workshop participants were shocked, but I simply asked the woman, "Why not?"

"Because," she said, "if I acted like that, all my friends would probably leave me. They like it that I'm such a good listener. They don't want to listen to me."

"Ah," I said, "so you want two things then: you want to be expressive and you want to be liked by your friends. Is that it?"

"Yes," she said, "but I can't see how I can have both."

"Try visualizing yourself," I suggested, "with friends who respect you for being expressive, who are happy to listen to you as well as have you listen to them."

She closed her eyes and imagined what I'd suggested. When she opened them a big grin spread across her face. "That's what I *really* want," she said. "To tell my story *and* have friends who listen and respect me for it. Thank you."

Another client wanted a recycling system for her home and office, but never quite got around to putting it in place. When I asked her, "Would you take it if you got it?" her answer was, "Only if it's simple and easy to use." I helped her revise her vision to specify what "a simple, effective, and easy-to-use recycling system" would look like. She had it in place within the week and it became an essential part of her life. Simplicity and success!

Sometimes you have to set priorities and choose between conflicting desires, at other times you can include all of what you want in your vision. Knowing when and how to do either is part of the art of creating that you develop through practice and experience.

10. Avoid Comparisons

Clients often have goals that include comparative statements such as "get slimmer," "have less clutter," or "have more money." These statements have little power because they are open-ended and lack clear criteria for success. They do not tell us "slimmer than what?" They don't specify a clearly recognizable end result. Thus, they lead to action that moves toward what you want, then away from it. As you get slimmer, the motivation to act fades. You quit doing what made you slimmer. You get less slim until you're again motivated to slim down.

Clear visions tell us exactly what we are going for. They enable us to recognize our results when we create them. Statements such as, "I would like to weigh "x" pounds," "wear a size x dress," or "have x-percent body fat," specify measurable criteria for success. The statement, "I'd like to be able to run five miles in thirty-five minutes, and still have energy left for dancing," specifies the result you want (the ability to run five miles), the criteria for success (in thirty five minutes), and how you would feel if you created it (energetic enough for dancing).

Comparatives also prevent you from seeing reality clearly and make it harder to consistently produce results. A few years ago, I worked with a client who directed a corporate fitness club. She'd listed "More money!" as one of the results she wanted to create. I asked her what that meant. She shrugged her shoulders and replied, "More money!"

"How much more money?" I asked.

"Just *more!*" she said, getting frustrated with me. I took a dollar from my pocket and handed it to her. "There," I said, "you've achieved your goal. You now have *more* money." She laughed and said, "That's not what I meant."

"Then what did you mean?" I asked.

She sat very still for a long while, then looked up at me and said, with unusual certainty, "$7,000 more a year!" She burst into a big smile, then added, "Jeez, I didn't even know I was going to say that. It just came out. But that's exactly what I want. $7,000 more will give me a salary of $25,000 and parity with other club directors in the industry." [*This was in the mid-80's.*]

"Ah!" I said, "So what you really want is parity with the other directors?"

"Yes," she said. "That way I'll know my employers respect me."

Her vision became *"A salary of at least $25,000 per year, tied to the industry standard, and a clear sense that my employers respect me and appreciate my work as evidenced by them giving me regular raises without having to ask for them."*

Once she'd crafted the vision, she was able to look at current reality more objectively. When she did, she noticed a large discrepancy between her and the directors of other clubs.

"They supervise more staff in their clubs than I do," she said.

"Why is that?" I asked.

"Well," she said, "most clubs have more members than mine, between 200 and 400 members. They need a lot of staff."

"Is your company smaller than the other companies?"

"No", she said, "we have the same number of employees as the other companies."

"How many members do you have in your club?" I asked.

"Fifty," she said, frowning. "Just me and my assistant run it."

"Does that tell you anything?" I asked.

"Yes," she said, "I need more members. Maybe I should organize a membership drive."

Working within the creative framework, she crafted a vision of a membership drive targeting the number of members she wanted to enroll. Then she looked carefully at her current reality, at what her facility looked like and what services it offered. To close the gap between vision and reality, she improved the locker rooms, added new services, and opened an hour earlier each morning. Over the next year, she tripled her membership. At her next performance review her boss praised her, recommended she hire another assistant, and gave her a fifteen percent raise. He also told her that if she had asked for another raise without showing results, he would have fired her. He had grown tired, he said, of hearing what he called her "victim story."

To her credit, this woman had shifted out of her victim stance into the stance of a creator. She told herself a *creating* story and acted on it. When I last saw her, her club was among the top three in the city and she regularly received raises without having to ask for them. She'd stopped obsessing about money. She realized that creating work that mattered was more important than chasing raises. Her life became simpler and more successful — all from shifting from a vague goal of "more money" to a vision that clearly specified the end results she wanted.

Using the Guidelines

These guidelines for crafting effective visions are not fixed rules that you must follow at all times. They are suggestions for making visions clear and compelling. They will help you craft visions that spur you to action and sustain that action until it produces final results. Do not take them as gospel truth; use them "as if" they were true. Try them out. Test them. Sometimes, for example, you can't include all of what you want in one vision, in one creation. Or you can't have all of what you want at one time. So craft two visions, of two creations. Create one result now, one later. Sometimes you might start creating without a vision and find that the vision emerges as you go. Jazz musicians do this when they "jam" together. There are no rules. Just guidelines, experiments, and learning from experience. If you make a bad decision, make another one. If what you do doesn't work, do something else.

Crafting a clear and compelling vision by using these guidelines may seem like a lot of work at first, particularly to those who see themselves as realists or activists. However, once you work with them, you'll see that vision crafting is an investment that pays big dividends down the road. It makes the process of assessing current reality and mapping out action steps much easier. It sharpens your focus. Most important, it is an essential step in setting up the creative tension that provides the motive force and energy needed to carry you through to completed results.

Alignment: Visions within Visions

Alignment is key in the creative process. Integrating simplicity and success requires that you craft powerful visions, carefully asses current reality, and make sure that your action steps align with and support what truly matters to you. When you're creating, it helps to have a vision for your whole life *and* for each result that matters. It helps to see how smaller results support larger results. This ensures that day-to-day actions have integrity. It ensures that they not only produce the specific results you want, but that together, those specific results add up to the kind and quality of life, work, and world that you most want. We'll look at the details of how you do this in Chapter 8. For now, I want to share an example of how I struggled to maintain integrity in my approach to creating simplicity and success.

After three years of trying to "be great" and "playing in the bigs," I decided to move to the island where I now live to see if I couldn't achieve more simplicity and still be successful. However, my life was divided into separate categories. On weekends, I dressed in jeans and fleece and hiked the ridges of the small mountains above my house. I joined the Nature Conservancy. I did Joe Dominguez's course on *Achieving financial Independence*. I wrote about simple living in my journal. But on Monday mornings, I'd put on a suit, catch a floatplane, and fly to the city to take on the competition in the " bigs." After a week of workshops, meetings, and consultations, I'd be worn down and frenetic. I'd fly back to the island, put on my jeans, and get back to living as I really wanted. I was out of alignment. My life was out of alignment. Then my Vancouver business partner told me he'd taken a job with another company. Without him, or someone like him, I knew I'd have to move back to the city and work even harder if I wanted to make it big as a consultant. But I didn't want to move.

One evening, while wrestling with my dilemma and watching the sun set behind the tall cedars across from my house, I flipped through old personal journals. I noticed how my vision and choices had changed over the years. What I thought was my most important priority had shifted from environmental education to simple living to outdoor leadership to personal mastery to corporate design and planning. A cold shiver that was part fear and part excitement ran up my spine when I realized that, regardless of whatever I'd put first, writing was *always* number two. Writing, I realized, was what I *really* wanted to do. Suddenly, everything fell into place. I knew what mattered. I would stay where I was and do whatever it took to create a simple yet successful career as a writer and a teacher. I'd focus on helping people shape rich yet simple lives that fulfilled their deepest needs for challenge and engagement.

As I'd done when I started Earthways, I lined up smaller visions in support of my vision of living simply and teaching people how to create. Those aspects that didn't align, I let go. I cut back corporate work. I started coaching over the telephone and via the Internet. I recorded my expenditures in a little book to see what my minimal monthly needs were. I planted a garden. I shopped at Value Village. Most important, I set aside time to write each morning and began working on this book. Immediately I felt the surge of personal power that comes when purpose, visions, and actions align. As I let go of my divided way of living, I experienced a deep sense of integration. I now feel like my life is all of a piece, cut from one cloth.

William Blake said, *"...one who would do good...must do it in Minute Particulars."* I've discovered that I create what matters in the same way, moment by moment, creation by creation. Knowing that the minute particulars of my life support and express my finest values gives me the confidence to press on in the face of adversity, setbacks, and occasional lack of resources.

A Cautionary Word On Visualization and Affirmation

"Vision without action," cautions a Japanese proverb, "is daydreaming."

Visualizing without a solid grounding in reality and action quickly becomes fantasy. On the other hand, focussing *only* on reality is likely to lead to reactive problem-solving. "Action without a vision," the proverb concludes, "is a nightmare."

Visualizations and affirmations are best applied within the creative framework. Visualizing desired outcomes adds power to a vision and heightens creative tension. Mental rehearsal can strengthen your actions. Affirming strengths, real capabilities, and actual achievements adds to your positive creative core and keeps current reality from being dominated by problems and limits. Be careful, though, not to affirm things that are *not* true.

There is a big difference between envisioning and choosing a result you want and affirming that you already have that result when you don't. "I choose to create a healthy, fit, and relaxed body," has a vastly different effect on your mind and brain than the statement, "I *am* healthy, fit, and relaxed" when you are *not* those things. The first statement adds to creative tension, the second one decreases it. Besides, affirming what is *not* true is a form of deceiving yourself. It erodes your sense of power and decreases your self-esteem. Who but a powerless person would have to lie to themselves to create results?

Visualizing desired results is a great way to add power to a vision. However, too many approaches stop there, implying or baldly stating that "holding a vision" is a sufficient strategy with which to bring into being what matters. It is not. In sports it's *not* the athlete who "holds the vision" the hardest who wins. The athlete who gets the gold is the one who best puts it all together on race day — vision, current reality, and action. It's the same in life. Holding a clear, compelling vision in your mind *is* a powerful and important skill, but it's not just vision that generates the power. The key to simplicity and success is not just holding a vision but rather holding creative tension. "Trust in God," says the Koran, "*and* tie your camel.

In the next chapter, we'll leave the lofty heights of vision and take a look at how to ground visions in reality. Then we'll see how these two forces, vision and reality, interact to form the framework for creating almost anything.

Chapter Nine

Grounding Vision in Current Reality

An accurate, insightful view of current reality is as important as a clear vision.

Peter Senge

Crafting a clear, compelling vision of a result you want is the first step in creating that result. However, it is not the only one. Remember that creative tension gives creating its power, not just vision. Creative tension is formed when vision is grounded in current reality.

When your vision is clear enough that you are confident you would recognize the result if you created it, the next step is to ask yourself:

- *What's the current reality of this result?*
- *Where am I starting from?*
- *What do I have in relation to the result I want? What do I lack?*
- *What forces are working in my favour? What forces are working against me?*

Knowing where you are when you start to create is as critical as knowing where you are when you begin a sailing journey. Imagine that you want to sail to Hawaii. If you think you're starting in Vancouver but you're really in Boston, you're likely to do more bumping into rocks and hard places than sailing. Without a solid grounding in reality, creating can be easily sidetracked.

Take Lydia, a single mom who told me that she worked so hard just to survive that she *never* had time to do the craft work that she hoped to make her living from in the future. "I work three jobs now," she said. "And I have to take care of my teenage daughter, who's become a real handful. I have no free time to myself. For anything!"

I had to admit that she looked haggard and seemed burned out. However, when I had her do a time audit, a detailed accounting of how she spent each half-hour of each day for two weeks, we were both shocked to discover that from six until eleven each evening Lydia lay on her living room couch and watched television. She had not counted this as "free time". Feeling so "wiped out" from her three jobs, she felt that she "deserved some veg time." "I just didn't realize," she told me when we examined the audit, "that I vegged so much."

This reaction is not uncommon. Many professionals and business people I've coached complain about working seventy to ninety hours. However, when they audit their time, most are shocked to find they work closer to fifty or sixty hours. "But," they plead, "it *feels* like ninety hours!" It may feel longer than it is, but feelings, important as they are to vision and to life in general, are not a very accurate way of evaluating current reality. Just because it feels like you work ninety hours does not mean that you do. Ironically, complaining that you work ninety hours can make you *feel* like you do work that much! It's a vicious circle.

After Lydia processed her time audit, she realized that she had thirty hours a week in which she could do craft work. I cautioned her to go slow; I sensed she still needed to veg a little. She agreed. She decided to start with an hour of craft work each night. She became more selective in her viewing habits and realized that she could do some of her prep work while she watched TV. Gradually, her TV time decreased and craft time increased. Her life opened up.

"Even though I do more now," she said a month later, "life feels simpler. It's less stressful, and more fun. I'm hoping that with income from my craft work, I'll soon be able to drop one of my part-time jobs." She also told me that, when she did watch TV, she enjoyed it a lot more.

Not As Simple As They Thought

Some clients come to me seeking validation and support for their approach to simple living. Although many *feel* that they already live materially simple lives, when they objectively assess their *actual* spending and consumption patterns in relation to their stated vision, values, and goals, they are shocked. They discover that they consume far more goods, services, and expensive experiences than they'd realized. Many don't even count what they spend on such things as restaurant meals, entertainment, vacations, and afternoons at the spa as consumption. As well, many realize that much of what they consume is unnecessary and unfriendly to the environment. Most important, they discover that the things that mean the most to them and that provide them with the most fulfillment, are often the things that cost the least — or nothing!

At first, the discovery that their lives are not as simple as they thought they were can be unsettling. Some try to deny it. Most of us do not like seeing current reality when it conflicts with our vision of ourselves. Not yet aware of the dynamics of the creative framework, many perceive the gap between vision and reality as a threat, something to be denied, or distorted in their favour. Gradually, though, these clients realize that if they want to create a simple, rich, and fulfilling life, it is critical that they assess their spending and consumption patterns objectively. They also realize that it's better to teach themselves reality than have reality force itself upon them.

To help them teach themselves reality, I have them record every cent they spend each day in a little notebook. At the end of each month, they sort their expenditures into categories and record the total for each category. So much for rent, so much for food, so much for entertainment, so much for car and gas, so much for clothing, etc.... Finally, they compare the amount that they spend in each category to the amount of fulfillment that expenditure provides them. Sometimes they decide to increase spending in an area because it would bring them more fulfillment. Often, though, they choose to reduce spending because an item costs more in life energy than it returns in fulfillment.

Time audits and spending records help clients assess their actions accurately and objectively. Similarly, healthy eating plans use food intake audits. Marathon runners keep track of their daily mileage, caloric intake, oxygen uptake rate, waking pulse level, and other criteria. Accurate records enable people to see where they are in relation to where they want to be. Learning to see reality as it is rather than as how you'd like it to be is not always easy. However, with practice, you get better at it. When you do, you are better able to set up creative tension and to take the action steps required to move you toward your desired results.

The following nine principles can help you accurately and objectively assess where you are in relation to what you want to create.

1. Be Honest with Yourself: Tell Yourself the Truth about Reality

To establish current reality as a foundation for creating, you must tell the *truth* about what happens. However, many, if not most of my clients have an adversarial relationship with reality. As Lydia did, they deny or distort current reality without realizing it. Rather than accept reality as it is, they argue with it; they demand that reality be as they think it *should* be. Insisting that reality is different from how it is not only makes it difficult to create desired results, it causes most of our emotional upset. "The only time we suffer," says author and reality-teacher Byron Katie in *Loving What Is*, "is when we believe a thought that argues with what is."[37]

Cognitive psychologists tell us that negatively distorting current reality is the basis of most stress, anxiety, and depression. Many of us deny or distort reality because we don't like what we see: pain, conflict, frustration, disappointment, injustice, unfairness, and circumstances that seem hopeless and unchangeable. Many of us would rather avoid the disturbing feelings that arise when, for example, we encounter homeless panhandlers. We disassociate ourselves from their plight because we don't know how to help. However, acknowledging such feelings brings them into consciousness and allows us to create appropriate ways of dealing with them.

We also distort reality because we don't like what it says about *us*. In *A Guide for the Perplexed*, E.F. Schumacher says that we tend to see ourselves and our own actions through the lens of our intentions, while we see others mainly in light of their actions. Of course, they see us through our actions and themselves through their intentions. This dual way of seeing reality causes much of the misunderstanding and conflict that occurs between individuals, groups, and even nations. It prevents us from seeing ourselves as others see us. It prevents us from grounding our intentions (vision) in the solid foundation of current reality. It also explains why we sometimes espouse one set of values yet act on a second, different set.

Researchers have found that there can be a dramatic difference between our " espoused values" — our intended values — and our "values-in-action" — the values we actually live by. I value compassion and gentleness. However, my reality includes a quick temper, which arises out of an habitual tendency to judge people too quickly. In spite of my *espoused* values of compassion and gentleness, I often act in ways that my friends describe as "edgy" or "prickly."

You might see this as hypocrisy. I prefer to see it as the gap between my vision and my reality. If I espouse compassion but deny my edgy temper, I get in the way of my good intentions. But when I recognize and accept reality as it is, I can dampen my temper and practice what I preach.

Some simplicity seekers I've worked with failed to see that, although they read simplicity books, attend simplicity workshops, and subscribe to glossy simplicity magazines, they really do not live a very simple life. This difference between espoused values and values-in-action goes a long way toward explaining the discrepancy between pollsters' predictions about a "transformation" to simplicity and how people actually behave. "Transformation," say Rosamund and Benjamin Zander in *The Art of Possibility*, "happens less by arguing cogently for something new than by generative action, ongoing practices that shift a culture's experience of the basis for reality." [38]

We simplicity seekers need to harmonize the values we espouse with the values-in-action that guide our day-to-day choices and behaviour. Learning to describe reality rather than judge it is an important step toward an integrated way of living.

2. Describe Reality. Don't Judge It!

Seeing reality clearly is the primary skill that enables creators to base their creations on a solid foundation. To show students how to draw the shapes they see, not the shapes they think they see, art teachers have students copy a drawing of a person. When I did this exercise, my drawing looked more like a child's stick figure than an accurate representation of the picture I tried to copy. I had drawn what I "thought" the person looked like. Then the teacher had us turn the picture we were copying upside down and draw each line in relation to the other lines. When I finished and turned my drawing right way up, I was shocked to see that it looked almost as good as the original.

Creators keep on good terms with reality. They do not fight reality; they embrace it, and then transcend it in favour of the results they want by taking creative action. You can keep on good terms with reality by *describing* it rather than *judging* it. To *describe* something is to state its characteristics, its appearance. Descriptions are best based on facts. To *judge* something is to form an opinion of it. Opinions are more like editorials than facts. They are stories we tell ourselves, interpretations. They get in the way of objectivity; they prevent us from clearly seeing what we observe. To objectively describe reality, we need to see what we see, without exaggeration or distortion, without making it better or worse, without adding opinion or interpretation. "The facts, ma'am, just the facts," Jack Webb urges witnesses on the TV cop show *Dragnet*. His advice applies equally well to teaching ourselves reality.

In my local workshops, participants see how judgments distort reality the first night. Although I keep my workshop room at 70 degrees Fahrenheit, someone inevitably complains that "It's too hot." As soon as they do, someone counters "No, it's too cold." To prevent conflict, I ask both to assess current reality by consulting a thermometer. Although they have different judgments about the temperature, they inevitably agree that it is 70 degrees. Then, because I realize that their subjective "feelings" are also part of their current reality, I suggest that the hot person lend his sweater to the one who is chilled.

When assessing current reality, it's best if you keep to the facts; don't spin out a story about those facts. For example, *I spilled red wine on my fiancé's mother's new white rug*, is a description of current reality. *I'm a clumsy idiot who doesn't deserve to get married,* is a judgment about reality. Negative stories can upset you more than reality itself.

The hole in the ozone layer has increased by fifteen percent over the last 12 months, is a description of current reality. *We only have ten years to solve the ozone problem or the damage will be irreparable,* is a judgment. Statements such as the last are predictions. They're made up to shock or frighten us into taking action by increasing the intensity of a problem or issue. But, in the end, they increase our sense of hopelessness and lead to inaction. If the world *is* going to end in ten years, then what hope is there? Instead of telling ourselves stories such as these, we're better off describing reality as it is.

3. Look Beyond Your "Concept" of Reality

Many of us make sense out of our lives and world by comparing what we see "out there" to the mental maps we carry around "in here." Mental maps include ideals that we impose on ourselves. They include theories and models of reality that we "believe" in. They include broad general concepts from science, religion, and philosophy that come to us from our culture. Added together, our maps, models, and concepts constitute a kind of mega-map or worldview, which we unconsciously label "the way it is." The tendency is then to see reality through the lens of our world-views. If you're a liberal, you see the world through that lens. If you're a conservative, you see the world through a different lens. Worldviews can compete with each other; arguments over what is "really" right can lead to conflict. We love our maps and models and don't want to give them up or change them. For many of us, they become more real than reality itself.

Scientist, philosopher, and founder of the field of *General Semantics* Alfred Korzybski cautioned that, "The map is not the territory." By this he meant that we should not confuse a map with the territory it depicts. The territory always includes more than our mental or physical maps can encompass. Although concepts help us make sense of reality, they can also distort it, especially if we mistake our map for reality itself. A menu is a kind of map of the food offered by a restaurant, but you wouldn't want to confuse the menu with the actual food.

Concepts simplify things for us by abstracting general data about reality while leaving out the specifics. When I drew my copy of the line drawing mentioned above, I drew an abstract representation — a concept — of what I thought a person should look like. I didn't draw what I actually saw on the paper in front of me. When I turned the picture upside down, my mind could not abstract a concept from the jumble of lines that I saw. Instead of my concept of an arm, I drew lines that inter-sected with other lines. Instead of my concept of a jaw, I drew an angle. Instead of drawing what I thought a nose should look like, I drew a curv-ing line and added some shadow. When I turned my drawing right side up — voila! — I'd drawn a very good copy of the original.

Although concepts are useful when you're crafting a vision, they can distort your perception of current reality. Mental maps may be badly drawn, inaccurate, incomplete, out of date, or just plain wrong. The concept "gentleman," for example, has changed greatly over the years. What was considered gentlemanly fifty years ago might now be consid-ered patronizing, sexist behaviour.

People with strong political, economic, or religious beliefs also tend to interpret reality in ways that fit with and reinforce their pre-existing beliefs and concepts. They choose aspects of reality that confirm their beliefs and strengthen their concepts. They leave out aspects that challenge them. While this makes for good arguments, it makes it difficult to get at the truth about current reality. Without that truth, it becomes almost impossible to create real and lasting results.

4. Include but Don't Exaggerate the *Positive* Aspects of Reality.

Being objective about reality means including the positive aspects of reality, all those aspects that work in favour of the result you want to create. Include the skills, resources, materials, and experience you already have. Revisit your positive creative core and include the confidence and competence that comes from doing so.

As you describe the current state of your result, look for evidence that you are "already there." Look for what is already in place. An author who wants to publish a collection of short stories or essays, for example, would include published pieces that are relevant to the proposed collection. "Already-there-ness" generates momentum. It makes it easier for the author to work on pieces that have yet to be written. Public speakers recall successful speeches to ground themselves in feelings of competence and confidence before speaking engagements. Doing so produces momentum that propels them forward. "Already-there-ness" also works for experiences that are only indirectly related to a result you want to create. Clients who have trouble imagining a simple yet successful life have less trouble when they recall the lives they led as college students. By assessing what made that simple time successful, they are better able to imagine a simple and successful future.

Although it helps to include what's already there, don't make reality out to be better than it is, at least not by much. Although research shows that modest "positive illusions" can be helpful in producing desired results, exaggerating the positive can distort reality. It makes it difficult to build a solid base upon which to create results. Worse, illusions sometimes become delusions.

Judy had recently divorced and was working full-time for the first time in her life. She asked to be included in an upcoming workshop but put off my request for a deposit. Finally, I asked her if she had money problems. "No," she scoffed, "I never have trouble with money. I just visualize what I need and it manifests." I doubted this was an objective assessment of reality, but Judy assured me it was. However, two days before the registration deadline, Judy's deposit had not arrived and others wanted her space, so I called her. I got no answer and no machine. This was strange, as Judy was in a business that required that she be in telephone contact at all times. I called throughout the weekend. Still no answer and no machine. I started to worry.

Monday, I called again. When Judy answered, she was sobbing and almost incoherent. I could tell she'd been drinking. When she'd calmed down enough to make sense, she told me she was completely broke. The bank had repossessed her car and foreclosed on her house. She'd exceeded her limits on both credit cards. Friday morning, she'd gone to the bank to request an emergency loan. The bank manager had not only turned her down, she'd recommended that Judy seek debt *and* personal counseling. She referred Judy to Social Assistance for emergency financial help. Judy was stunned. When she told her teenage daughters she was going to Social Assistance, they packed their things and went to stay with their father. Bewildered and overwhelmed, Judy had started drinking Friday afternoon and hadn't stopped all weekend.

"How could this happen?" she sobbed over the phone. "Every day, in every way, I try so hard to succeed. How could *this* happen?"

It happened because Judy exaggerated the positive aspects of her financial reality. In her Pollyannaish attempts to put a positive spin on her situation, she so distorted reality that she truly believed she could create money merely by visualizing it — even as her deteriorating finances told her she could not. It's fine to be optimistic about reality, but distorting it to make it look better than it is can backfire as it did on Judy.

5. Include but Don't Exaggerate the Negative Aspects of Reality

When clients first assess current reality as part of the creative process, many have a tendency to focus on negative aspects. Perhaps they are still stuck in problem-solving, which focuses predominantly on negative things — problems! Moreover, many problem solvers take an overly pessimistic stance toward reality. Pessimists think that their difficulties are *personal, pervasive,* and *permanent.* They think adversity is their fault, that it will affect their entire life, and that it will probably always be the way it is now.

Although research shows that pessimists see reality more objectively than optimists, an overly pessimistic explanation makes reality seem worse than it actually is. Often, pessimists try to manipulate themselves (and others) into action by envisioning then reacting to negative scenarios. By exaggerating the negative aspects of current reality, they create a reactive, fear-driven impetus to act. This strategy, however, can backfire. Andrew, an ambitious but stalled executive from Seattle, called me one day to say he'd decided to end our coaching relationship. He was angry with himself and frustrated with his lack of progress. I asked him to explain what he meant. I thought he'd been making excellent progress in all areas of our work.

"I'm just not getting it," he said. "I'm not having *any* success. This week, for instance, I didn't do *any* of the things I set out to do. *None.*"

I asked him to get out his list of choices — projects he'd committed to act on. I had a copy that he'd faxed to me. "What about the first one?" I asked, "That seemed straightforward."

"Oh," he said, "I did it, but it was such a small thing, I didn't count it."

"What about the second one?" I asked.

"Well, I did that one too. But it was really nothing."

"And the third? The fourth? The fifth?"

"Yes. I did them, but again, they were pretty straightforward."

Although I disagreed with his opinion of the difficulty of those tasks, I let the comment go.

"What about the sixth and seventh?" I asked. "They kind of went together, didn't they?"

"Yes. I did the sixth and have just about finished the seventh."

"And the eighth?"

"Just about done."

"The ninth?"

"I just need to send it to the printers."

"And the tenth?"

"Well, that's just it," said Andrew, his voice rising plaintively, "that's the problem. I didn't do anything on it. Not a thing. It makes me so mad. I had all week and I didn't even look at it."

I asked him if he was telling the *whole* truth, that he "didn't do a thing" on the tenth result.

"Well," he said, "it was the most difficult, so I put it off until yesterday. Then I just roughed out a draft and gave it to a colleague to look over. I didn't get very far. I'm not even half-way there on it." I started to reply, but he interrupted, "But the point is I *didn't* finish it. I *didn't* do as well as I could have. That's what upsets me so much. I feel like I've failed."

Andrew had completed six of the ten things he'd committed to do that week and most of three others, yet felt that he'd failed. Part of his difficulty came from focussing exclusively on what he had *not* done — the last half of his last task — and not giving himself credit for what he *had* done. Another part came from using feelings as his primary measure of progress. Because he told himself that he'd failed, Andrew *felt* like he'd failed. Then in typical vicious circle dynamics, he used his feelings to justify his judgments. "Why would I feel like I'd failed if I hadn't," he asked.

I explained how thoughts give rise to feelings, how the stories we tell ourselves about reality upset us more than reality itself. I showed him how negative judgments distort reality and give rise to negative feelings. Andrew understood the concept, but something deeper seemed to prevent him from seeing reality clearly. After a half-hour of gentle probing into the structure underlying his negative opinions, Andrew shared a story from his childhood. In it, he described his father berating him for not trying hard enough in a foot race at a school sports day.

"Dad sat me down after the race and lectured me," Andrew said. "I didn't hear most of what he said, but I do remember him saying over and over again, 'You didn't give it all you had. Anything less than a hundred is zero.' All these years later, anytime I come up short, I still hear his voice ringing in my ears. 'Anything less that a hundred is zero!' I call it the *Voice of Judgment* — the *VOJ* — and it freaks me out every time."

Andrew had taken a boyhood injunction to try his best and turned it into a rigid policy by which he judged his adult results. He believed he had to be perfect or, in his mind, he'd failed. After all, anything less than a hundred was zero. I helped him see how his judgment affected his ability to describe reality objectively. I suggested that saying "I completed eighty percent of the tasks I set out to do, but still feel frustrated that I didn't finish them all," would be a far more honest, accurate, and empowering statement than "I didn't do a thing."

It is fine to include feelings as *part* of current reality. Just don't make them your primary standard of measurement for how well you're doing. You can be doing well, making good progress, and still feel badly about it. I also see clients who are *not* making progress but "feel" that because they feel good they're doing great. They usually end up frustrated and disappointed.

Andrew saw that his policy-driven judgments distorted reality and created emotional tension. Although it wasn't easy for him, he worked at assessing reality more accurately. The coaching session occurred nearly ten years ago, yet I still get an occasional call from him when he needs help with current reality. Old habits die hard. Be careful what you tell your kids!

6. Try to Stay Away from Absolutes

Statements such as, "It's *impossible* to live simply in the city," or "There is *nothing* I can do to make my community a better place," or "I'm *always* doing dumb things" do not accurately describe reality. They judge it. Moreover, they are judgments based on absolute generalizations.

This is not nit-picking semantics. The language we use to represent the world becomes our map of the world. If our language is inaccurate, our map is inaccurate. If we rely on a faulty map, we are not likely to end up where we want to go. When assessing reality, be careful that your descriptions do not contain absolute words such as *all, any, never, ever, nothing, always, totally, completely, impossible, etc.*... Your assessment of reality will be more accurate when you avoid these words, or qualify them with phrases such as "sometimes," "almost," or "mostly," etc....

Absolute words carry a high emotional charge. They trigger emotional reactions in you and others and lead to misunderstandings and conflict. Avoiding trigger words is particularly important if you are trying to co-create results with others. We've all no doubt experienced variations on the following conversation between spouses.

"Did you take the garbage out this morning?"

"Oops! Sorry, I forgot. I'll do it now."

"Don't bother. I already did it. Like I *always* do."

"Like you *always* do?"

"Yes! I *always* have to take it out because you *never* do."

"That *is* a damned lie. You *are* a liar. I take it out nearly *every* day."
And the fight is on!

There are two things going on here. First, using the words "always," "never," and "every" distorts reality. Such absolute judgments make reality out to be worse than it is or better than it is. They obscure the truth, trigger defensive reactions, and make finding common ground all but impossible. Second, using the verb "to be" in the forms "is" and "are" also absolutizes aspects of reality and leads to further anger and defensiveness.

7. Beware of the Verb "To Be"

Statements that begin "It *is*...," "You *are*...," "I *am*...," tend to be dogmatic. For example, a self-assessment such as "I *am* lazy," is quite different from one such as "I don't like to work on things that have little meaning to me." The first is an absolute judgment. The second is a description. Absolutes make categorical statements about how you *are* and thus imply that you will always be that way. Descriptions state that you act in certain ways under certain conditions.

When describing current reality, it is best to avoid the verb "to be" and its various forms. Any of us who've taken a parenting course have learned not to say things like "You are a good girl, or you are a bad boy", but rather, to describe the behaviour we want. "I like it when you're gentle with your brother, Susie." "Billy, when you hit your sister with your airplane, it hurts her, and makes me want to take it away from you."

Similarly, in couples counseling and communications courses we learn not to make "you" statements because the you is usually followed by a judgmental "are," as in "You *are* a liar." Instead, we're taught to make "I" statements such as, "When you say that you "always" take out the garbage, I get confused and feel angry." Avoiding the verb "to be" helps us keep current reality clearer and makes it easier for us to create the results we want.

8. Never Underestimate the Power of "Yet"

Earlier in my career, I directed a mountaineering school and adventure based executive program in the Rockies. Although not much of a climber myself, I coached participants in applying *creating* skills to challenging and sometimes frightening situations.

Ninety percent of our participants were men and most were highly competitive. Often, because they used their arms rather than the stronger leg muscles, some men would experience failure. Their fingers would slip off a hold and they'd fall back onto their safety rope. Driven by a competitive desire to succeed, they'd try repeatedly, only to burn themselves out. Exhausted and frustrated, they'd reluctantly let themselves be lowered off the rock on the rope. Since such a "failure" is difficult for hard-charging executives to accept, they'd react with self-loathing, anger, and defensive judgments about reality. "That move's *impossible*," they'd say. Or, "There's *no* way I can do that."

I responded to such statements by gently but firmly saying, "Yet!" Then, I'd point out that "I *can't* do it" was a judgment, not a description of reality. Moreover, it was absolute. It implied that "not only can I not do this now, I'll *never* do it." The fear that they'd never succeed terrified these men. (That, and the deeper fear that their buddies *would*.) I'd also point out that all they really knew was that they could not do the move at this time or in the way they'd been trying. Maybe, I'd suggest, they'd do it tomorrow, when they'd rested. Or when they'd practiced more. "Or maybe," I'd propose, "there's another way you could try it."

I'd ask one of our women instructors to climb the route because, having less arm strength, they intuitively used their legs. As the instructor glided easily up the route, a client would note how she made the angle less steep by keeping her hands inside a corner and her feet outside it. Someone would notice, "She's not using her arms except for balance." When she'd completed the climb and lowered off, I'd ask the client if he'd like to have another go at the route.

"Try it Sharon's way," I'd suggest. Almost always, they'd succeed. They'd come down, satisfied and surprisingly humbled. They'd smile sheepishly and say, "You were right. I couldn't do it *yet*." Such successes built momentum and helped clients take on more challenging routes. Without the "yet" lesson, some might have quit. In the course wrap-up, the executives reported that the "yet" lesson was one of the most useful they'd learned all week. They saw how it applied throughout their personal, professional, and organizational lives.

You don't have to climb rock faces to learn how to apply the power of "yet." In workshops, I ask people to think of something that seems impossible. What they imagine could be anything: doing spreadsheets on a computer, running six miles in under forty-five minutes, drawing human faces, making flaky pie crusts, fitting into a size six dress, bench pressing 250 pounds, making a soufflé that doesn't fall, whatever....

Once they select something, I ask them to imagine themselves trying it but not being successful. I ask them to see themselves failing at it. Then I have them say, "I cannot do that," and note how they feel. Almost everyone reports feeling "down," "depressed," "frustrated," "despairing," "hopeless," or "like giving up." Their body language shows deflation and defeat.

Then I ask them to visualize exactly the same situation again, to imagine themselves trying something they want to do and not succeeding. This time, I ask them to say, "I cannot do that *yet*." When I ask them to note how they feel, they report feeling "pumped," "hopeful," "excited," "motivated," "committed," "like I should practice more," or "maybe if I got some coaching...?" They sit up straighter. Their faces are more alert. Most smile excitedly. Adding "yet" to "I can't do it" opens up the challenge; it adds hope and possibility.

Hope is critical in creating. With it, momentum becomes easier to build. When people lose hope, they either give up and quit, or they force themselves to change by imagining negative scenarios and reacting to their fear of what might happen. "If I don't get this project done on time, I'm gonna get fired." "If we don't solve the environmental crisis by Friday, we're all gonna die." This is conflict manipulation. It is the opposite of working toward a vision. It negates vision.

"Without vision," says the Bible, "the people will perish." So does scientist David Ingvar. He's a neurobiologist who studies brain function with the aid of PET scans that show computer-generated pictures of the neo-cortex during different states of mind. He found that parts of the brain turn off when individuals cannot anticipate a positive future.[39] When, for example, evangelistic environmentalists tell us that we have only ten years to totally change our way of life or we and the Earth will die, many simply throw up their hands in frustration or duck out for a beer. In the face of such overwhelming negativity, our own small efforts seem puny. Making unfounded generalizations and judgments about how bad reality is can make reality seem overwhelming and hopeless. Action seems futile. However, not acting leaves us feeling helpless, even hopeless, and even less likely to act. It's another vicious circle.

Adding "yet" to judgments about our competence to cope with reality can build hope, spur us to action, and generate the momentum needed to get us through difficult times. A judgment like, "We don't know how to live simply and in harmony with our environment," can lead to despair. Add "yet" to that statement and it leads to hope, and to learning, experimenting, and creating what you need to know in order to live simply and in harmony with the Earth.

9. Keep Your View of Reality *Current.*

Finally, it is important that you assess current reality *continually.* Time lags in your feedback systems can make creating difficult. Think about those old showers where you turned the hot water tap and nothing happened, so you turned it some more then suddenly got a blast of scalding water. That's a system with a feedback lag. Reality constantly changes. Don't *assume* that it remains the same as it was the last time you looked. We all know how embarrassing it can be to have an ATM machine tell you that you don't have sufficient funds when there's ten people in line behind you. A big part of assessing current reality is keeping that assessment current.

Although reality changes, there is no reason to make change an enemy. If the forces of change divert you from your path or blow you off course, all you have to do to keep creating is clarify your new position (your new current reality), compare it to your vision, and then choose the best next steps to move you toward the results you want.

Even if you aren't blown off course, it helps to remember that each action you take alters the relationship between vision and reality. Seeing that reality has changed will influence the next steps you take. Feedback allows you to make adjustments, take new actions, and move closer to what you want. Even small actions, over time, can have a large effect. If a spacecraft traveling from Earth to the moon were only one degree off course, it would miss the moon by thousands of miles. You need to keep your observations current and up to date. Current reality means current!

Creators do best when they see reality clearly and without distortion, when they describe it as honestly, accurately, and objectively as they can. When reality is perceived objectively, it becomes neutral, free of emotion. The place for emotion, for passion, is in vision. Vision then becomes a more powerful force than reality. Tension between vision and reality is more likely to resolve in favour of the result you want to create. So remember that reality is not the enemy. You can teach yourself reality or you can let reality teach itself to you. I suggest that you get on good terms with reality rather than react to it. Besides, wouldn't you rather know the truth about reality than tell yourself a distorted story about it?

Crafting a clear, compelling vision then grounding it in an accurate objective view of reality sets up the basic framework of the creative dynamic. The discrepancy — the gap — between vision and reality gives rise to creative tension. In the next chapter, we'll explore how to use creative tension to create results that matter.

Chapter Ten

Creative Tension:
The Engine of Creativity

(T)he gap between vision and current reality is a source of energy. If there was no gap, there would be no need for any action to move toward the vision. Indeed, the gap is the source of creative energy. We call this gap creative tension.

Peter Senge

Just as vision by itself does not comprise the whole of the creative process, neither does merely adding current reality to vision. At the beginning of Chapter 2, Christopher Childs stated that a "field of creative energy" is set up by "accurately representing the world of today while stubbornly holding out a genuine vision of a better future." The key word in that sentence is "while." While *simultaneously* holding vision and reality in mind, creators set up *creative tension*. Although we looked at the basics of creating and resolving creative tension in Chapter 2, we'll now look more closely at this powerful engine of creativity.

To set up creative tension, first imagine a result that you want to create. Then, imagine the current reality of that result. Finally, visualize vision and current reality together as if they were projected on a split screen. You might place your vision above and reality below with a gap between them. Or place them side by side: vision on the right, current reality on the left. Visualize them as if they were snapshots that capture the essence of the two states. Still pictures enable you to focus more clearly on what you want and what you have than do moving pictures.

Once you can see both vision and reality simultaneously, allow yourself to imagine a force arising out of the gap between them. Let yourself feel a gentle, pleasant tension, like that of a stretched rubber band, the pull of a magnet, or an attraction to some place or person. Hold that tension gently in your mind. Learning to hold creative tension is the most important and the most powerful skill in creating. Sometimes, you will resolve it quickly. Other times, you may hold it for years. I've held the creative tension out of which I crafted this book for over five years.

Experiment with visualizing vision and current reality. My own practice has become three-dimensional. I see my vision up to the right and out in front of me. In the left, lower foreground, I see a snapshot of the current state of my vision. In between — stretching out, away from me, and up to the right — is a gap in which I feel a tangible tension, a dynamic force.

Although some people feel creative tension the first time they try the split screen exercise, most do not. Creative tension is easy to describe but not as easy to master. To master the skills of setting up and holding creative tension and living comfortably with it, you may need to practice.

Three Ways to Resolve Creative Tension

You use the energy of creative tension to take action. However, not all actions resolve that tension in favour of the results you want to create. There are three ways to resolve creative tension:

1. **Give up**. Let go of your vision and the tension will resolve toward reality.

Without vision, current reality drives the action. You react or respond to problems, circumstances, and outside events. The results you produce are often temporary solutions, not the creations you most want to bring into being. The parable of the fox and sour grapes is an example of this scenario. Sacrificing vision for others is another. Many women from my mother's generation gave up their dreams to support husbands and families and saw those dreams wither like fruit on a stunted vine. Unless you understand how creative tension is created and can see its place in the creative framework, you are likely to confuse it for emotional tension and seek relief. Of course, doing so, as we've seen, rarely leads to real and lasting results.

2. **Compromise.** Split the difference between vision and current reality. Let your goals erode; be fuzzy about reality; make only small changes. While this may appear to be a good strategy, it rarely produces real and lasting results.

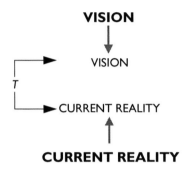

In this scenario, you settle for less than what you truly want. Partial results may be produced, but, because compromise is rarely satisfying and tension is reduced, the framework eventually breaks down. Current reality again drives the action. Couples who don't love each other, but stay together "for the sake of the children" often fall into this kind of a scenario. So does the individual who wants to be a poet but settles for being a copywriter because s/he wants the security of a regular paycheque and to look successful. We'll examine the compromise strategy shortly.

3. **Create.** Hold vision firmly in tension with current reality; assess current reality accurately and objectively; and then take action to change reality so it moves toward vision.

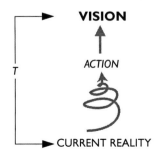

In this scenario, vision drives the action. Creative tension is strong. You orchestrate its resolution toward desired results by making strategic decisions and taking actions that support vision. Because the creative process is rarely a linear, straight-line progression from current reality to completed vision, don't feel that you have to control the process. Creative tension sets up a container for creativity, a field of possibilities. Once you establish creative tension and hold it gently yet firmly in your mind, you can be open and flexible. You can play with the possibilities. You can experiment, try things out, and see what emerges. With creative tension energizing and guiding your actions, it is easier to work with the forces in play. You can make changes in reality that move you in the direction of your vision. Sarah's story about her dream cottage is a great example of an individual working within this framework.

When I have creative tension set up, I feel excited, energized. I feel a pull to action, an urge to experiment, a desire to play with the forces I meet. Sometimes, as it was with Sarah, the tension is so powerful that I can't *not* go with it. I am swept up in creative flow, left only with the option of joyous, creative surrender. In "flow" we become focussed. Thinking and doing are integrated. Vision and reality interact to form creative tension. Simplicity and success become one. Positive psychologist Mihaly Csikszentmihalyi describes the flow state in his book *Finding Flow*:

> When goals are clear, feedback relevant, and challenges and skills are in balance, attention becomes ordered and fully invested. Because of the total demand on psychic energy, a person in flow is completely focussed. There is no space in consciousness for distracting thoughts, irrelevant feelings. Self-consciousness disappears, yet one feels stronger than usual. The sense of time is distorted: hours seem to pass by in minutes. When a person's entire being is stretched in the full functioning of body and mind, whatever one does becomes worth doing for its own sake; living becomes its own justification. In the harmonious focussing of physical and psychic energy, life finally comes into its own.[40]

Creative tension is radically different from psychological or emotional tension. It is a useful motivating force. It feels good. Emotional tension, by contrast, is the anxious, uptight, panicky, sometimes angry feeling that comes from fearing and failing to accept some aspect of current reality. It can also come from not being able to live easily with the gap between vision and current reality. When you feel open, flowing, expansive, eager to move toward the result you desire, that's creative tension. When you feel closed down, up tight, and fearful, that's emotional tension.

When you experience emotional tension, use it as a signal that you've slipped out of the creative process and are probably dwelling on some negative aspect of current reality. To get back into the creative flow, re-establish creative tension by focussing on vision and current reality together. See your emotional tension as a part of current reality. Acknowledge it, accept it, but don't dwell on it. Instead, expand your focus to include both your negative emotions and your vision. Acknowledge the gap between vision and reality; allow yourself to feel the creative tension emerging from that gap. Once you have creative tension established again, take whatever action seems appropriate to you. If you decide to do something about emotional tension, you're more likely to do so in a way that also supports your vision of what you want to create.

Tolerating the discrepancy between where you are and where you want to be is a necessary skill for creating what matters. A low tolerance for *creative* tension leads to *emotional* tension. It prevents you from living easily in the gap between vision and reality. Holding a clear vision *and* an accurate view of reality but *not* holding them together does not work. Vision energizes and excites you, but current reality discourages and depresses you. Stuck between the two, you feel emotional tension. Actions and energy are diverted to seeking relief from your negative emotions. Real results are not produced. Eventually, you give up, give in, or burn out. Or, perhaps, seek a compromise as a way out of emotional tension.

Compromise: The Tragedy of Eroding Goals

Creators sometimes use compromise as a step toward what they most want. However, they never see it as an end or goal. Their goal is always the creation of the result they want to create. Creators do not drop their visions to make things easier or to accommodate problems and difficult circumstances. They do whatever it takes to bring the creation into being.

Early in his career, author Ken Follett conceived an idea to write a generation-spanning novel about the building of the great cathedrals in the Middle Ages. However, his ability to describe buildings was not a match for his vision. He put the idea aside while he wrote thrillers such as *Eye of the Needle* and *Lie Down With Lions* to hone his skills. He also spent years exploring cathedrals and developing his vocabulary of descriptions. In 1989, he published *Pillars of the Earth*, a captivating, epic story about a family of medieval cathedral builders. It became an instant best seller. It stayed on the *New York Times* list for over eighteen months and was on the German best seller list for six years. Follett still sells 100,000 copies a year! Putting aside an idea that moved him deeply while he developed the vocabulary, experience, and skill to do it justice can be seen as a kind of compromise. To Follett it was an action step that supported his vision.

If, instead of committing to your vision, you let it slip a little each time you face difficulties, your vision can shrink to nothing. Peter Senge calls this process the "eroding goals syndrome." He says people who lower their goals to make success easier gradually become less successful. As do companies and organizations. "The dynamics of eroding goals," says Senge, "lies at the heart of the demise … of many American manufacturing industries."[41] By dropping standards, settling for less, many manufacturers failed to produce quality products and went out of business.

Eroding goals also explains why many individuals and groups fail to create what they want. Individuals who let their vision of integrity slip to accommodate circumstances become less honest with themselves and others. Small businesses that settle for doable results rather than stretching for what matters become less meaningful to their owners, harder to sustain. Schools that let standards slip lose quality students and staff, which causes their standards to slip further.

Although compromise can be a useful step toward a vision, when it becomes an end in itself, the power of creative tension is lost. Imagine if Bach or Beethoven had compromised on their great symphonies, or if Jane Austen had settled for a romance novel format to share her insights on love and life. Imagine what your life might become if, instead of quitting or compromising in the face of difficulties, you maintain creative tension and keep moving toward your vision.

Do What You Love

Many clients come to me for coaching because a compromise approach to life and work has not delivered the results they *most* want. These clients appear to be successful, at least by conventional standards. Most are professionals and business people who *do* produce results — just not the results they *most* want. They sacrificed their deepest longings and highest aspirations for material symbols of success — money, cars, fancy homes, and pricey toys — hoping that status, respect, and satisfaction would come with the possession of such symbols. Lacking a clear map of the creative process and unable to establish creative tension, they felt forced by circumstances to do things other than what they loved. To make money, achieve respect, take care of their families, or sometimes just to survive, they compromised. Many thought that if they worked hard, saved money, and achieved financial freedom, then they could do what they *really* wanted.

However, instead of moving toward what truly mattered to them, they became fixated on a narrow definition of achievement. Money became their measure of success. They lost sight of their deeper values and higher dreams and failed to create the results they *truly* wanted. Tragically, most of them also failed to save much money because they spent too much on the expensive symbols of success, and on strategies for getting relief from the stress and anxiety that came from doing work they didn't believe in or care about.

Michael Phillips, a simple liver and author of the *Seven Laws of Money* recommends against this "save now, do what you want later" approach. His first law of money urges you to do what you love. "Do it!" he says, "Money will come when you are doing the right thing."[42]

Phillips is not some wild-eyed, new age fanatic. He developed the *MasterCard* concept and was a co-founder of *The Briarpatch*, a group of successful, ecologically responsible San Francisco businesses. He suggests that we separate our dream from the challenge of survival. As well as urging us to "do what you love," he suggests that we also pay attention to reality. Do what you must to stay alive, he urges, but "...a person's focus must be on his passion." Even if you have to wait tables, drive taxi, substitute teach, take care of other people's kids, or even manage a large corporation to keep food on the table, you should keep your *predominant* focus on your dream, on your passion. By doing so, you will be successful in both process and result.

Money, Phillips suggests, should always be seen in a secondary role, supporting your passion. Don't wait until you have enough money before you start making your dreams a reality, do it now. When you're doing the right thing, money will come.

Living Easily In the Gap

History is replete with examples of creators who overcame a lack of funds and difficult circumstances, or both, to focus on their passion. Van Gogh sold only one painting in his lifetime, yet he left an amazing legacy of work. Ray Bradbury wrote 1000 words a day for ten years before he sold his first story. (If you're an aspiring writer, read that last sentence again!) Thom Jones was a janitor for eight years before he published his stunning book of short stories, *The Pugilist at Rest*. Academy Award-winning actors tell of waiting tables for years before breaking into films full-time. Many Olympic athletes work part-time at a large hardware chain.

These examples show compromise in the service of vision rather than compromise as an end. If you have to compromise by working at a "day job," realize that such a compromise is a step in the greater process of producing your long-term results. I find that when my clients get in touch with their passions and clearly envision the results they most want, they find it much easier to accept, even enjoy their day jobs. They find it easier to organize jobs so they support their passion. Many find it easier to cope with low incomes, and even to save money when they're focussed on a vision of what truly matters. Many enjoy this simple, focussed way of living so much that they maintain it even after they've become financially successful.

Holding the Tension

Some people think that vision is all they need to produce results. Simplistic positive thinking and affirmation approaches encourage this "hold the vision" approach. These "willpower manipulation" approaches work, but only for a short time. If what you affirm is not true, reality will eventually rear its objective and forceful head and make itself known. Merely holding the vision does not set up creative tension or lead to results. Indeed, it often backfires.

I once tried out a sales program in which I had to look myself in eye in the mirror each morning, then smile and repeat, *"I am the best salesman in the world,"* fifty times. At first this was pleasant and uplifting, but one morning, when I was tired and a little discouraged, the little reprobate that lives in the attic of my mind flipped open the trap door and shouted down, "Oh nooo, you're not! If you were, you wouldn't have to stand there every morning doing this silly exercise." That little reprobate was telling the truth. Although I wanted to succeed at sales, I was not yet good and definitely not *the best.* Telling myself that I was the best only reinforced my doubt and confusion. Who but someone who isn't a success has to tell himself that he is?

Positive thinking and affirmations can be useful tools. They work well when celebrating actual results. However, affirming what is *not* true distorts current reality. It destroys creative tension and prevents you from creating what you want. The sad irony is that those who use affirmations to *will* what they want into being usually fail to affirm small steps and successes. They judge actual results as less important than the results they affirm. Focussed on willing change through affirmations, they ignore a critical momentum-building part of current reality.

Why Choice Has More Power than Affirmation

The statement, "I *choose* to create 100 widgets this month," does not set up a contradiction or conflict when juxtaposed with the statement, "I now create five widgets a week." It simply highlights the gap between current ability and my aspirations. It sets up a creative framework and generates creative tension. Working within the creative framework, I can use that tension to take action, develop new skills, explore new techniques, make new contacts, and do whatever I can to stretch toward my desired results. However, juxtaposing the affirmation "I am the best salesperson in the world" with "I sold five units this week" leads to conflict. Instead of generating creative tension, it sets up cognitive dissonance or what Robert Fritz calls an "ideal-reality conflict."[43] When I affirm conflicting statements, something has to give. Unfortunately, it's often the truth.

I find it ironic that many authors who recommend affirmations also warn their readers about the evils of denial. They don't seem to realize that lying to your self about current reality *is* a form of denial. No matter what you call it, lying almost always backfires. Remember Judy, who thought she could manifest money. Had she accepted her ordinary self, she might have taken appropriate actions to keep her finances in working order. Affirmations that are not true make it almost impossible to accept yourself. Eventually, the little reprobate that lives in the attic of your mind will throw open that trap door and confront you with the truth. Worse, reality might ram the truth down your throat, as it did to Judy, forcing you to see what is real and what is not.

Your Ordinary Self is Good Enough

Your ordinary self *is* good enough. To create what you want, you do not have to be anyone other that who you are. You are as you are and might as well accept it. Accept means "to receive willingly." Instead of affirming what is not true, you'd do better to focus on a vision of what you want, willingly accept reality as it is, set up creative tension, and then take action.

Please don't misunderstand. I'm not saying that you shouldn't visualize what you want or affirm successes and positive actions. You should. Recognizing and affirming successes on your way toward creating the result you want is essential. I'm simply saying that because creative tension is the engine of creativity, it is critical that you separate your vision of what you want from an objective assessment of what you currently have. It is possible, for example, to have a vision of being a successful salesperson (or anything else) while you're still learning the ropes. "Acting as if…" can be a useful strategy — if you're clear about vision and honest about current reality.

Acting *as if* you're successful and confident can give you confidence. When you show confidence, others will have confidence in you. You are more likely to be successful than if you appeared self-effacing and fearful. I used this technique when I first began speaking in public and putting on workshops. In spite of my dire fears that people would reject what I had to say or laugh me off the stage if I made mistakes, I *chose* to present myself "as if" I were a $10,000 a day presenter. I walked on stage with my head held high, a smile on my face, and performed the role of a confident expert. Over time, and with practice, experience, and a pattern of successes under my belt, my competence increased. I became confident in my work and myself. I grew into the role I once had to perform. So long as this tactic is embedded in the creative framework, it serves you well. However, if you lose sight of reality and forget you're playing a role, it can backfire. If you start to believe that you *are* a top presenter before you've developed the skills, experience, and grace that top presenters embody, you're more likely to appear arrogant than confident.

Two Great Forces

Many people stumble through life without vision, driven by a reality they define as an enemy. Henry David Thoreau captured the essence of this sad, struggle-filled existence when he said, "The mass of men lead lives of quiet desperation." Creators transcend this struggle by harnessing two of the most powerful forces we know — *love* and *truth*.

"In order to create there must be a dynamic force," claimed composer Igor Stravinsky, "and what force is more potent than love?" By crafting a clear, compelling vision of something you truly want, you tap into the power of love. A vision of something you would love to see exist acts as a beacon, drawing you toward it. Such love is a beautiful thing; so is truth.

"Beauty is truth, truth beauty," said poet John Keats. You tap into *truth* by grounding vision in current reality. Being objective about reality you make it a neutral force. You strip it of its power to negatively affect your emotions. Indeed, studies show that the most consistently effective form of therapy — cognitive behavioral therapy — is based on the simple insight that it is our thoughts, our interpretations, and the stories we tell about reality, not reality itself that causes distress.

Love and truth. Creative tension harnesses both in the service of what matters. Yet many of us shy away from them. We tell ourselves that what matters doesn't matter. We tell ourselves we're not good enough, that we don't have what it takes. We're even afraid of our own power. Here's how Marianne Williamson addressed this fear:

Our deepest fear is not that we are inadequate,
Our deepest fear is that we are powerful beyond measure.
It is our light, not our darkness that most frightens us.
We ask ourselves, who am I to be brilliant, gorgeous, talented, and
fabulous —
Actually, who are you not to be?
You are a child of God.
Your playing small doesn't serve the world.
There is nothing enlightened about shrinking so that other people
Won't feel insecure around you.
We were born to make manifest the glory of God within us.
It is not just in some of us: it is in everyone,
And as we let our own light shine, we unconsciously
Give other people permission to do the same.[44]

When we tap into love and truth, we let our light shine. We become the person we glimpse during peak experiences or moments of flow. When we work *with* the forces of love and truth, we come into our own power. Not "power over" but rather power with forces in play. Empowered by the ability to create, we are better able to realize our own greatness and the wealth of natural possibilities that exist in us and in the world we live in.

The power to consistently create the results that you dream you can create comes from clearly envisioning what you deeply love. It comes from acknowledging reality as it is. It comes from living comfortably with the tension that arises out of the gap between vision and reality. Mostly, it comes from choosing what you want to create and taking action to bring reality into line with the result you envision.

In Chapter 8, we'll examine the place and power of choice in the creative process.

Chapter Eleven

Choice in the Creative Process

We become truly human only at the moment of decision.

Paul Tillich

Much of the complexity in our lives is involuntary complexity. When we react to problems, we focus on what bothers us, not on what we want to create. When many bothersome things occur, we feel like a pinball, constantly bounced from problem to problem. Life is complicated, confusing, and often more complex than we can handle. We feel as if we are at the mercy of external forces, forced to do what circumstances dictate. This is far from the bright and powerful life envisioned by Marianne Williamson. Until we master our own creative process, many of us live such desperate lives. Without a framework for integrating vision, reality, and action, it's difficult to order decisions and choices around what matters to us.

We've begun to put such a framework in place in the last three chapters. Envisioning results and grounding vision in current reality sets up the framework and generates creative tension. Although that tension provides the energy to create, it does not, by itself, generate results. To activate creative tension's power, we must consciously *choose* the results we want to create.

Choosing Results

Choosing is fundamentally different from wanting, wishing, hoping, or affirming. Moreover, it's more powerful. Think of something you want but don't yet have. Visualize it and say to yourself, "I *wish* I had it, I *hope* I get it, I *already* have it."

Where is the power in those statements? Within you, or external to you?

Now visualize your result, and say to yourself, "I *choose* ...(and fill in the blank with the result you want to create)." Where is the power in *that* statement? In you!

Which has more power? "I wish," "I have," or "I *choose*"?

Choosing is a deliberate step toward creating what you want. It sets the direction for your future. When you consciously choose to create a result, you do not have to force anything. You do not have to exert willpower. You do not have to affirm that you already have it. Instead, when you choose to create a result, you access your own creative power. Moreover, when you act, the Universe acts with you.

Some people do not consciously choose what they want. They hope for it, wish for it, or ask others to provide it for them. I've had clients who practiced affirmations such as, "Everyday, I'm getting better and better," but never made the conscious choice *to be healthy*. Focussed on getting rid of disease, their actions were reactive problem-solving, not creating.

You can't always create what you want, but you can make a space out of which it can emerge. Setting up creative tension and then choosing the results you want to create greatly increases your chances of bringing those results into being. When you fail to choose what you want, you give your power over to external forces. You're in danger of being swept along by circumstances, buffeted by the slings and arrows of adversity.

Creators transcend circumstances and adversity through two kinds of conscious choice.

Formal Choices

By envisioning results and then grounding them in reality, creators establish a framework that guides their choices and actions. Although not as formal as a strategic plan in which all the steps are laid out in advance, the creative framework sets up a hierarchy of choices in which less important choices are organized so they support more important choices.

Although I have many results that I want to create, I usually have only a half dozen that are major enough to formally commit to the creative framework. While I occasionally rough out projects on the back of an envelope, I map out major results using multi-level charts that I post above my desk. That sets up my creative framework. After that, much of my creating and choice-making is done moment to moment. Before I describe that informal process, let's look at how making formal choices can generate energy and commitment.

In an instructors workshop, Robert Fritz had us make a list of everything we wanted, both personally and professionally, from now to the end of our lives. He then asked us to pair up with another person and have them ask about each result we'd listed, "If you could have that, would you take it?" (You don't need a partner for this; you can ask yourself the same question.) If the answer is *no*, cross the item off your list or change it to something you do want. If the answer is *yes*, then formally choose that result by saying aloud, "I choose ..." (and fill in the result you want to create). Do this with each item on the list. Then take a moment to savour the feelings that come with formally choosing what you want. Most people report feelings such as "lightness," "freedom," "liberation," "personal power," and "increased energy."

Hierarchies of Choice

Creators know that different choices lead to different kinds of results. They know that some choices are more important than others. Creators work with at least three kinds of choices, each of which has a strategic place in the creative process. To simplify choice-making, they set up layered or nested systems — hierarchies of choice — in which *foundation*, *primary*, and *secondary* choices are integrated within a dynamic structure.

During the age of political correctness, the concept of hierarchy was discredited. The evils of certain types of hierarchies were generalized to all hierarchies. Ironically, opponents of hierarchy judged non-hierarchical approaches superior to hierarchical approaches. In doing so, they unwittingly arranged the two approaches in a hierarchy of value. Hierarchy *per se* is *not* bad. Our bodies, natural systems, indeed, most of the world is arranged in nested hierarchies. Atoms combine to form molecules which combine to form proteins which combine to form muscles, etc... all in hierarchies, or if you prefer Arthur Koestler's term, *holarchies*: nested systems of wholes within wholes within wholes.

Riane Eisler, author of *The Chalice and the Blade* urges us to distinguish between *dominator* hierarchies and *actualization* or *growth* hierarchies. Dominator hierarchies are rigid social structures that oppress people and groups. Growth hierarchies align and integrate individual actions into fully functioning systems. As Ken Wilber says in *A Theory of Everything*, "growth hierarchies convert heaps into wholes, fragments into integration, and alienation into cooperation."[45] Creators arrange choices in growth hierarchies. Such nested systems order and guide their choices so that they consistently support the results the creator wants to create.

Foundation Choices

Foundation choices are basic life orientations to which creators commit. They include choices such as the choice to be *free*, to be *healthy*, to be *true to yourself*, to be *happy*, to be *the predominant creative force in your own life*, to *live simply yet richly*, to *live lightly on the earth*, to *live in harmony with the principles of your faith*, to *be open to the presence of Spirit*, or any other choice about something of fundamental importance to you.

Buddhists, for example often choose to dedicate a sand painting, a meditation session, a meal, or even a new day to their own enlightenment and to the enlightenment and benefit of all beings. They make their choice formally, in a brief private ritual, before taking action. Making these kinds of choices consciously and deliberately creates a foundation upon which *primary* (result) and *secondary* (action) choices rest. Experiment with making the foundation choices that have power and meaning for you. Doing so could have a major effect on your creative process.

When clients such as Celia and Al report that they are not making progress, I ask, "Are you making your foundation choices every day?" Ninety percent say, "No." Many people go on diets, take supplements, and eat health foods, yet fail to make the foundational choice to be healthy. Others take workshops, read self-help books, and spend years in therapy, yet fail to make the foundation choice to be true to their highest selves. Initially, Celia and Al downshifted, cleared out clutter, and simplified the material aspects of their lives but failed to make the foundation choice to live a life of deep and enduring simplicity. Therefore, many of their choices were merely to get rid of what they *did not* want. Much of their effort was wasted because what we resist persists! Clutter, whether it's stuff or stress, comes back.

To make foundation choices, go back to the list above and sit with it for a few minutes. Don't force the choices on yourself, just try them out, and see which fit for you. Then formally choose by saying to yourself, "I choose to be free." Note how you feel. Note whether that choice fits. If it does, make it every day. Try out other choices. Formally choose those that have the most power and resonance for you. Then make foundation choices part of your daily practice of creating. Once you know which choices you want to make, it takes less than a minute. I make mine in the tub or on my morning walk. Doing so grounds my whole day in what matters.

Making daily foundation choices aligns your entire being in support of what is most important to you. It is easier to stay on track when you have a firm foundation beneath you. You are able to adapt to change and deal with conflict in ways that not only solve immediate problems, but also move you toward desired results. When Celia and Al resumed making foundational choices, they reported that their choices and actions became more integrated and aligned. Primary and secondary choices were easier to make. They started making progress again.

Primary Choices

Primary choices are about specific end results, creations you want to create for their own sake. A painting is a primary choice for an artist, not just a step toward career success. It is something she loves and wants to see exist. It might also contribute to her career, but that is not her primary reason for painting it. A gold medal-winning performance is a primary choice for an athlete. A fit, healthy body can be a primary choice. For Celia and Al, work that supported their foundation choice to live a simple yet engaged life was a primary choice.

Some choices are both. For some painters, a commissioned piece is both an end in itself and an important career step. A magazine article might be an end in itself for a writer and a chapter in a book-length memoir. For followers of Joe Dominguez's and Vicki Robin's *Your Money Or Your Life* approach, "FI" (Financial Independence) is both an end in itself and a step toward the simple, yet fulfilling life those practitioners long to live. Wholes within wholes within wholes!

You always have more visions of results than you can work on at one time. A vision does not become primary until you *choose* to create it. When you designate a result a primary choice, you commit to bring it into being.

On Commitment

Scottish mountaineer W.H. Murray captured the essence of commitment when he described a critical point in the 1950 Scottish Himalayan Expedition. Even before they left Scotland, the expedition encountered numerous difficulties and setbacks. Uncertainties surrounded it. Expedition members were not sure whether to go or stay. Finally, they decided to make the expedition a primary choice. They committed.

"We put down our passage money," said Murray, "booked a passage to Bombay".

"This may sound too simple," he added (in a paragraph that you may have seen mistakenly attributed to Goethe), "but it is great in consequence. Until one is committed there is hesitancy, the chance to draw back, always ineffectiveness. Concerning all acts of initiative (and creation), there is one elementary truth, the ignorance of which kills countless ideas and splendid plans: that the moment one definitely commits oneself, then Providence moves too. All sorts of things occur to help one that would never otherwise have occurred. A whole stream of events issues from the decision, raising in one's favour all manner of unforeseen incidents and meetings and material assistance, which no man could have dreamt would come his way. I have learned a deep respect for one of Goethe's couplets:

> *Whatever you can do, or dream you can begin it.*
> *Boldness has genius, power, and magic in it.*"[46]

Secondary Choices

Having committed to their primary choice by paying for their passage, the Scottish expedition members then made *secondary choices*. They ordered supplies, developed climbing strategies, arranged for overland transportation, and began training for the challenge ahead. Later, on the mountain, they made more secondary choices, all of which flowed from their original decision to commit to Everest as a primary choice.

Secondary choices are action steps you take to bring your primary choice — your creation — into being. A painter experiments with colour tones so she can capture the subtlety of her vision. Athletes get up at 5:00 AM to train because it supports their vision of a gold medal. Participants in a *Simplicity and Success* program track daily expenditures so they know where to cut expenses and increase fulfillment. Environmental supporters buy unbleached paper and organic cotton clothes, grow organic vegetables, and recycle as steps to support a sustainable life and community.

The primary-secondary hierarchy makes managing daily choices and actions simpler than reacting or responding to circumstances. When you commit to primary choices, it is easy to make strategic action choices. *Secondary choices* always *support primary (result) choices.*

Creative Moments

Throughout the day, we face moments when we have to choose between conflicting courses of action. Such *creative moments* are strategic; they are critical in the creative process. They are the moments in which what we envision becomes real, the moments in which we shape the lives, families, relationships, work, and world we most want. It is at creative moments that we become most fully human. They often happen so fast, that there is no time to invoke formal choice-making processes. We have to make such informal choices on the fly, in the moment.

Whenever things are not going as you'd like them to go, ask, "Why am I doing this? What primary choice does this decision or action support?" Practice this *Creative Moment* exercise:

1. Notice what is going on. Note what you're saying to yourself about the situation, other people in the situation, and yourself. Ask, "Am I describing what I see, or judging it? Is the story I'm telling myself helpful? Is it the truth? Will it help me move toward what I want? Or will it lead to conflict, seeking relief, or giving up?"

2. Focus on your positive creative core. Recall times when you were in similar situations. Remember when you performed well,

when you transcended difficulties and produced results you wanted in spite of the circumstances or problems you faced.

3. Focus on the result you want. Envision what you want to create. Separate what you want from what you think is possible.

4. Formally choose the result you want by saying, "I choose...."

5. Move on. Take whatever next steps occur to you. Take a break. Go for a walk. Take in a movie. Make some notes in your journal. Call a friend. Or go back to what you were doing when you got stuck and try again.

When you do this exercise, you will often notice that your initial response to circumstances was not a conscious choice. It was a *reaction*. Making good choices can be challenging in the heat of the moment. But practice and experience can build this skill so that it becomes automatic.

After several weeks of practicing the *Creative Moment* technique, Sheila told a workshop group how it might have saved her marriage. Her husband Don rarely shared in housework, although they both had full-time jobs. Don's one concession to domestic duty was to do the laundry. Because he did it on Saturdays and hurried home to watch "the game," he often put the clothes away damp. Later, Sheila would pull a white blouse out of a drawer only to find an ugly mildew stain growing across the front of it. She told us that she'd tried to explain her frustration. She'd tried to get Don to understand that clothes had to be totally dry before he put them away. But, he always argued, they *felt* dry when they came out of the drier. One Saturday Sheila met Don at the door as he returned from the laundromat. "Did you dry them completely?" she asked.

"Of course," he said.

She slid her hand into the pile of clothes to test them. They were damp. "I almost lost it," she said. "I was so angry. I pulled my fist back and was ready to pound him when I remembered the Creative Moment stuff. In a flash, I asked myself, "What do I want?" *A loving, respectful relationship with my husband.* "Would punching him help?" *No.* "What would?"

"All this took place in the blink of an eye. Don saw me pull back my arm. His eyes flared. He started to pull back from me. In that instant, I chose to love him and to show him that I did. I put my arms around him, and kissed him. He was stunned. I whispered in his ear, 'They're still damp, honey.' Don's eyes were wide open, his jaw hung down, but he didn't say a word. He turned around and went back to the laundry. I never found mildew on my clothes again."

Sheila realized that loving Don was a higher order choice than clean blouses. She was able to act from that hierarchy in the heat of a difficult moment. Not only did it save her marriage, she said, but the experience and the learning that came from it helped her succeed in other parts of her life. Don was so impressed that he decided to take the workshop himself. Together, Sheila and Don went on to become highly proficient co-creators.

"Things are simpler now," Sheila told me later. "And much richer. Both of us have become focussed and successful. Don got a promotion. I just got national recognition for one of my projects. Yet we still seem to have more than enough time to do things together. Most incredible, Don now gladly does his full share of the housework."

But What If I Want Two Things?

Creating hierarchies of choice is different from traditional goal setting. It is not enough to merely list things you want. Some things *are* more important than others. You need to be clear about what is primary, and what is secondary. To make effective choices, focus on your primary choice, make sure you're clear about current reality, and then arrange your secondary choices — your actions — so that they support your desired result. Sounds easy. Yes?

But what if you want to be trim and fit *and* want to eat a dozen fresh, honey-glazed donuts?

No problem! See it as a creative moment. Shift your focus from your hunger — or from your desire to experience momentary pleasure, or get relief from emotional conflict, or whatever drives your desire to eat donuts — to your higher-order desire to have a healthy, fit body. Imagine how you'd look, how you'd feel, and how proud and happy you would be if you realized that vision. Then decide which is most important: eating the donuts or having a fit, healthy body? Most of the time you won't eat the donuts. If you do, see it as an experiment. Note the results and make any needed adjustments. Like, say, taking a two-hour walk?

Throughout our lives, we are continuously challenged by conflicting desires. Work or leisure? Money or love? Spouse or children? Friends or family? Success or fulfillment? The list is endless. Creating hierarchies of choice eliminates much of the conflict surrounding such choices. It helps you transcend such dilemmas. It increases your effectiveness, adds to your confidence in difficult situations, and, as do all the core creating skills, it greatly increases your chances of producing the results you want. In almost every way, hierarchies of choice will help you simplify your life and create the kind and quality of success that you most want.

Co-Creating Hierarchies: Another Couple's Success

Creating hierarchies of choice is particularly important when you want to co-create results with others. If knowing what to want is, as Geoffrey Vickers said, "the most radical, the most painful and the most creative act of life," knowing what to want in concert with others is that much more radical, painful, and creative.

David and Beth took one of my workshops together. During the workshop, each of them worked on individual creations as well as co-creations around which they shared a mutual interest. The most significant of these involved a vision of getting married, moving from the city to a smaller, more rural center, having a family, and living a simpler, more focussed life. After the workshop, each came to me for individual follow-up coaching. During a session that occurred following a business trip to Hawaii, David shared something that was troubling him.

"I'm not sure about the 'getting married' part of our vision," he told me. When I asked him why, he said, "In Hawaii, I realized that I'm still attracted to other women."

"Have you told Beth this?" I asked.

"No," he said. "I could never tell her that. It would hurt her too much."

I pointed out that Beth's reaction was her business not his. Trying to control her reaction, albeit with what he thought was her best interest in mind, was a form of manipulation. "Besides," I asked, "How do you know it will hurt her? Wouldn't you want to know if she was attracted to other men?" David reluctantly acknowledged that he would, but still didn't want to tell Beth.

Later, during a coaching session they attended together, it became apparent to Beth that David's commitment to their vision of getting married was less solid than hers.

"Couldn't we just move out there and stay as we are?" he asked. "Living together works fine."

"It works fine as long as long it's just you and me," said Beth. "But if we're going to have children, Dave, I want to be married."

I pointed out that the root of their confusion seemed to be a lack of hierarchy in the primary choices that made up their vision. "What is the most important aspect of this vision?" I asked.

Beth immediately answered, "Having a family." David said, "They're all important."

After more probing, David realized that if he had to rank his choices, having a family would be most important. "Would it be safe to say," I asked, "that as well as being primary results you want to create, moving to the valley, getting married, and living a simpler life are also secondary choices that support your higher-order vision of having a family?"

"Yes!" they both answered.

I turned to Dave. "Does that make a difference to your feelings about getting married?"

"Yes," he said, "but..."

"Is there something else that you'd like to share with Beth?"

David glared at me. Then he took a deep breath and turned to Beth. "I'm worried about getting married," he told her, "because I'm still attracted to other women."

Beth smiled and said, "And you think that's news to me?"

"You knew?" David said.

"You've always had a roving eye," she said. "You don't intend to do anything, *do you?*"

"No," he said. "I just like looking."

"So, look. Just don't touch."

Within six months, David and Beth sold their house in the city and moved to acreage just outside a smaller city in a lovely, interior valley. A year later, their son Daniel was born.

Integrative Power

Arranging choices in a mutually agreed upon growth hierarchy gave Beth and David the power to create together. In a November 1978 article in New Age magazine, "Women and Power," Patricia Mische described this kind of co-creative power as "integrative power."

"As power *with* the other," she said, "it does not benefit one at the expense of the other or the community, but tends to benefit both self *and* others. It is a caring form of power. It is power aligned with love. It is the combination of both power and love that makes a good marriage or family life workable. It is this alignment of love and power that is essential to shape a humanizing future — on a personal level and in the world."

Creating and maintaining a hierarchy of choices within the creative framework is a key to creating and co-creating results that serve both individual and group needs. It is a key to crafting simplicity and success. It is a powerful tool for co-creating the kind and quality of marriage or relationship you want. Or family. Or business team. Integrating action choices with results choices is far more likely to produce lasting results than seeking balance or compromise.

Once you know how to make choices, you can direct the resolution of creative tension toward what matters. Following the path of least resistance set up by the creative framework, you can take action that naturally and organically moves in the direction of what you most want.

What could be simpler? What could be more successful?

In the next chapter, we'll look at how action steps unfold in the creative framework, and how to build momentum toward completed results.

Chapter Twelve

Action Steps:
The Art and Craft of Creating

I long to accomplish a great and noble task, but it is my chief
duty to accomplish small tasks as if they were great and noble.

Helen Keller

In the creative process, small tasks combine with other tasks to yield more than the sum of their parts. Mozart may have conceived symphonies on afternoon walks and then written his scores in ink, but most creators don't work that way. Most work more like Beethoven, creating results through a series of small yet integrated steps. That's also the way most of us craft simple, successful lives — step by step by step. Gradually, our small steps add up to the life we long for.

Two Kinds of Action

Once you establish a creating framework, generate creative tension, and are clear about your hierarchy of choices, there are two kinds of action to take: *direct* and *indirect*.

Celia prefers direct action. It is formal and strategic. She writes out elaborate descriptions of her visions and their relevant current reality. She charts out strategic steps so that realistic goals, secondary choices, and action steps line up with her vision. She specifies success criteria for her primary result and the secondary results that support it. Then, secure in her framework, Celia explores the possibilities that occur to her. She tries out actions and then analyses their effects. She updates current reality regularly. She takes new actions based on the new relationship between vision and reality.

Al is more casual. He prefers an indirect, free-flowing approach. Rather than carefully sketch out vision, he's content with a vague, visceral sense of what he wants. He quickly checks out current reality, then dives into action, following his nose, going where intuition leads him.

Much of the time he appears to be doodling, or noodling, or just dozing off. Often his best ideas or actions pop into his head when he's working on another project.

Most creators combine both approaches. For long-term creations, they favour the direct approach. When focussed on short-term results, they stay in the moment and use the indirect approach. Although creators may prefer one approach to the other, they do not become attached to one at the expense of their results. If one process fails to support their results, they choose another. They do not glorify process at the expense of their creations.

Regardless of which approach you prefer, you don't need to know all the steps before you start. You don't need to lay down rigid plans and strategies in advance. Once you have creative tension, all you need are your next few steps. Taking those steps increases your experience, adds to your skill and knowledge, and helps you decide what steps to take next. With each step, reality changes, often in ways that are impossible to plan for. The path emerges out of the doing. However, if the doing is not contained within a guiding structure, it can become overly complex, even chaotic. When he applies his casual approach to long-term projects, Al is often frustrated by a lack of progress and slip backs into problem-solving, trying to force results into being.

Telescoping End Results

There is a way to combine the structure that Celia prefers with the process that Al likes. Robert Fritz developed a simple yet strategic way to integrate goals and actions.

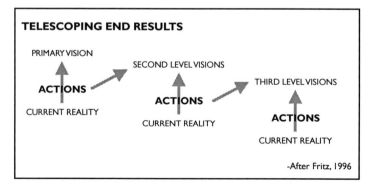

TELESCOPING END RESULTS

PRIMARY VISION

SECOND LEVEL VISIONS

THIRD LEVEL VISIONS

ACTIONS

ACTIONS

ACTIONS

CURRENT REALITY

CURRENT REALITY

CURRENT REALITY

-After Fritz, 1996

Fritz's planning approach works down from higher-order purpose and primary goals to concrete, local goals and actions. Out of the simple elegance of the repeated, fractal form of the creative framework emerges a complexly structured map of primary, secondary, and tertiary choices. "Complexity as well structured as this," says Fritz, "is relatively easy to manage."[47]

One of my clients is simplifying and focussing her life by creating a wellness-promotion business that expresses her finest values. The business, *Avenues to Wellness*, is Louise's primary vision. It includes a whole-person Wellness Program, Yoga instruction, and Journal Writing workshops and retreats. When she began, none of those things was in place. Developing them became strategic action steps in her primary vision chart. Because those steps were also creations that she cared about and wanted to bring into being, Louise developed second level charts for each of them. One of the action steps in the second level chart for the Wellness Program was "professional-looking, easy-to-follow workbooks." That, too, was a creation she cared deeply about. It became a third level vision and she developed a chart for it.

"It seemed like a lot of hard work at first," Louise said, "but once I'd done it, I could clearly see how everything fit together and how all the small steps supported my larger goals. Once I'd done my charts, everything seemed to flow more easily. What had seemed almost overwhelmingly complex when I tried to hold it all in my head seemed simple, elegant, and doable when I charted it out and got going on it."

The diagram on the next page illustrates how another client charted out the action steps for an ecologically designed cottage he wanted to create.

Co-Creating Desired Results

In a life, a career, a marriage, a group project, and even a business or an organization, telescoping end results establishes the form of the creative framework as the predominant planning structure. It provides a common protocol and easily understood language for dealing with issues or conflicts so that actions lead to results, not reaction. It aligns people at all levels of a group or organization around the goals and visions of the group. Even those farthest removed from the top or the

TELESCOPING END RESULTS
Mapping Out Vision, Reality and Action Steps

Desired Result:
An Ecologically Designed Cottage

Vision of Desired End Result:
- 1200 square foot, solar-heated, post & beam cottage overlooking a meadow leading down to a lakeshore beach.
- 2 bedrooms and a den with small, efficient fireplace
- Cedar decks off front, back and master bedroom
- Glass solarium with plants across sun-facing front
- All materials sustainably produced and non-toxic
- Organic garden for veggies and flowers.
- Detached writing studio at edge of lake

. . . .

- Have Dave do basic plan, then cost out
- Draw up rough sketch of house
- Increase savings to $25,000 in 10 months
- Contact agents in areas of low cost
- Research housing costs in different areas via Net

Current Reality:
- Living in 1200 sq. ft., rented apartment in town.
- Paying $950/month rent and utilities.
- No deck or balcony. o Noisy.
- Have $16,000 in savings, take home $2500/mo.
- Job as free-lance writer is transportable
- Have computer, fax and modem. Internet access.
- Working 1/2 to 2/3 time

.

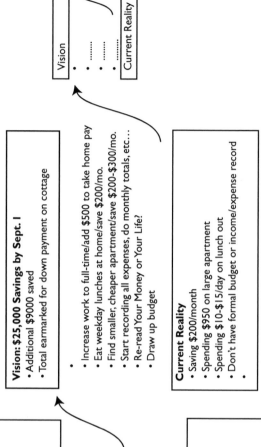

Vision: $25,000 Savings by Sept. 1
- Additional $9000 saved
- Total earmarked for down payment on cottage

- Increase work to full-time/add $500 to take home pay
- Eat weekday lunches at home/save $200/mo.
- Find smaller, cheaper apartment/save $200-$300/mo.
- Start recording all expenses, do monthly totals, etc...
- Re-read Your Money or Your Life!
- Draw up budget

Current Reality
- Saving $200/month
- Spending $950 on large apartment
- Spending $10-$15/day on lunch out
- Don't have formal budget or income/expense record

.

Vision
. . . .
. . . .
. . . .
Current Reality

Integrating Values and Action
Applying the practices of creating within the framework of the Creative Framework allows you to integrate and align a great number of variables. This makes it easier to ensure that your day-to-day decisions and actions consistently support the primary results you want to create and the higher life/work purposes to which you aspire.

centre can easily see the relationship of their small action steps to the grander visions, purpose, and mission of the organization.

Telescoping is a way to map out the relationships between actions and results and between results and larger results. It's not a rigid plan that must be followed. Producing results changes current reality. When reality changes, you sometimes have to change course and develop new action steps. To facilitate ease in making these kinds of adjustments, I write out my new action steps on large *Post-It* notes and stick them on my charts. Fritz and his colleagues have developed special computer software with which you can prepare and update your charts.[48]

Alignment between actions and goals also aligns employees, teams, and divisions. Eventually organizations that use this approach begin to resemble symphony orchestras or a jazz ensemble with all the players working in harmony. The same occurs in smaller groups, even families. It's a way for you to organize your life so that the music of your soul is more easily expressed. It's a way of transcending complexity and achieving the simplicity on the other side of complexity.

Railways or Sailboats?

In a creator's world, *invention* takes precedence over *convention*. Unlike so-called strategic planners who lay out elaborate plans in advance and then try to stick to them regardless of shifts in current reality, creators operate on a more just-in-time basis. Within the creative framework, they telescope end results and then focus on next steps, get started, and keep moving. They experiment, learn from mistakes, adjust actions, and build momentum toward results. Failure becomes simply feedback. Current reality shifts in response to both successes and failures as well as to outside events and perturbations. New assessments of reality pinpoint current position. Course corrections are made immediately. The plan emerges out of the doing.

Creating is more like ocean sailing than taking a train. On a train trip, you not only know where you'll start and where you'll end; you also know the exact route and all the stops in between. The route is fixed and inflexible, albeit predictable. When you're sailing, your route is open and changeable. All you know in advance is where you're starting from and where you want to end up. The route you sail will be influenced by the forces you encounter during your trip. Winds, tides, currents, storms, other boats, mechanical problems, and the unpredictable inter-actions among these variables make detailed planning difficult if not impossible. Instead of rigidly following a detailed plan, sailors make up the route as they go.

Sailors are more flexible, better able to deal with change and difficult circumstances than train-takers. When sailors are blown of course they get out a sextant or tune in their GPS and determine their current posi-tion. They set their compass heading for an appropriate course toward their destination. Then they turn the tiller and head off on their new course. Compare this to what happens when a train goes off the track!

Sailors draw energy from external forces by working within a frame-work that includes a desired destination and a carefully plotted daily posi-tion. Creators do too: they keep their vision foremost in mind, they know at all times where they are in relation to their end result, and they work with the forces in play to invent the route from where they are toward the result they want.

Once creators have set up the creative framework and established creative tension, they are free to experiment, explore, and let the path of least resistance emerge. Along the way, they do what is needed to bring their vision into reality. And most do so without a detailed plan. Indeed, creators know it can often be harmful to work out the whole path from vision to results in advance.

The Perils of Over-Planning

"Although planning," an insightful observer remarked, "is essential; plans are often useless." That's because plans too often become ends in themselves rather than tools for action. Their purpose is forgotten or ignored. People stick to plans even when current reality changes. As a *Strategic Design* consultant for businesses and organizations, I see the negative results that arise from thinking that *The Plan* is more important than an on-going planning process.

In many organizations, plans take precedence over ends. Most plans are made for, not by, those charged with carrying them out. Rigid adher-ence to policy takes precedence over flexible innovation and invention.

Keeping to the plan becomes more important than achieving results. In such organizations, much of management's time, energy, and resources are spent enforcing plans and policies rather than providing those who do the work with the tools, information, and support to do their best in the simplest, most effective ways. In such a climate, over-cautious employees and managers protect their flanks. While they faithfully follow *The Plan*, high level goals get lost in rigid adherence to details. Real and lasting results are not produced.

Individuals who over-rely on goal-setting and planning approaches that lack the framework and dynamic tension of the creative process often find themselves in the same conundrum. Clients come to me because they cannot follow the elaborate plans they paid consultants large sums to prepare. The plans they show me are carefully crafted. The difficulty is that they are all about goals and results; they contain nothing about current reality or what do when current reality changes. So the clients find themselves in the difficult position of either scrapping their expensive plan or forcing themselves to follow it in spite of changing reality. Neither option serves them well. I help them ground their career goals in current reality. I show them how to work within the creative framework to set up the tension-charged container for creating. I show them how to take experimental action and make up a plan as they go. Almost always, this turns out to be a more successful process than following a predetermined plan. In work, as in life, the simplicity on the other side of complexity is both elegant and rewarding.

Realistic Goals

Sometimes *creating* is criticized for being "too visionary" or "not realistic." Such comments usually come from those who don't understand the process and the framework in which creating unfolds. When I speak to high school kids, I urge them to stretch for what truly matters, whether or not they believe it is possible. However, teachers often intervene to stress the importance of realistic goals. They counter my advice with their own about setting "doable" goals.

I understand their intentions, but I don't see this as an either/or issue. In the creative process, there is no dichotomy between visionary and realistic goals; there is alignment. Although vision and visionary goals are key to the creative process, realistic goals serve as important secondary choices and action steps. If a vision is large and complex, it is critical to set strategic, doable goals as benchmarks with which to measure your progress along the way. Athletes integrate increasingly more challenging goals into their creative framework. Although their overall focus is a championship or gold medal, at any given moment they focus on their next sub-goal, such as "to make the finals." Well-coached athletes focus on creating their best possible performance each time they compete. In spite of focussing on one event at a time, these athletes understand the relationship of doable goals to their larger vision. Again, it's a matter of wholes nested within larger wholes, etc.... Athletes are keenly aware of the holarchy they set up and where they are within it as they focus on their next goal.

Creators know that circumstances (current reality) can change at any time and are prepared to set a new course, to establish a different holarchy of goals and action steps. Anton, one of my clients who played the piano well, wanted to realize a life-long vision of playing professionally. He gave himself two years to achieve his goal and then set a series of nested goals with which to measure his progress: master a basic repertoire of pieces; play for gatherings of friends; volunteer to play at friend's parties or weddings; then play for tips in a local cafe or coffeehouse. He saw these interim goals, not as a plan to follow, but as benchmarks by which he could mark his progress. As it turned out, he hardly followed the steps he set out.

Once he told his friends about his two-year plan, one of them asked Anton to play at his wedding. Playing at the friend's wedding landed him a regular, three-nights-a-week job at one of the best restaurants in town, paying him more money than his day job. Anton changed his list of results choices and action steps to include teaching improvisation techniques. He hoped that would help him generate all his income from piano-related work. Just over a year later, he quit his day job. His planning helped him see a way to bridge the gap between vision and reality, but Anton was smart enough not to stick to his plan when reality changed. He charted a new course, took new action, and jumped to a new level of competence and confidence. Anton's life became simpler and richer. Content to do what he loved, he no longer felt compelled to purchase unnecessary consumer goods to make himself feel better. Although he hadn't intended to become a simple-liver, he did.

When you create, you plan as you go. You make up the process as you move toward vision. When you harness creative tension, every action has a tendency to move you toward desired results. Even setbacks and mistakes add to the tension, making your next action more likely to succeed. Taking action, noting results, correcting mistakes, and building momentum through more action teach you how to create your result. Gradually you bring the results you want into being.

BARRIERS TO GETTING STARTED

Getting started can be the most challenging part of creating. Inertia is a powerful force to overcome. There is comfort in remaining where you are. It is risky to venture into the unknown. Fear of failing is a major obstacle to getting started; so is fear of succeeding. Sometimes you fear both at the same time. I often had difficulty working on this book. Inertia arose out of my fear of failing, of putting time, effort, and the sweat of my brow into the project and then having it rejected. I also feared that if the book succeeded, I might fall prey to arrogance, take on too much, and become mired in involuntary complexity, no longer living the simple, enjoyable life I loved.

When either of these fears surfaced, I grounded myself by focussing on my positive creative core. I scanned for times when I'd overcome similar fears and produced results I wanted. Then I recommitted to my vision, assessed my current reality objectively, and took whatever action occurred to me. I hope you think that my efforts worked.

Still Another Variation on the "Yeah, but…" Syndrome

Getting started is particularly hard for some because, rather than hold vision and reality as interacting components in a creative framework, they hold them as opposites.

*"I want to write, **but** I have no talent."*

*"I want to eat more ecologically, **but** I don't know how."*

*"I want to work on my relationship, **but** my partner is not cooperative."*

When you hold vision and reality as opposites, they cancel each other. You lose creative tension because a structure of opposites wants to go in two directions at once. Emotional tension builds. You shift back and forth between the two poles rather than move consistently toward desired results. Your focus shifts to seeking relief from the emotional distress you feel.

You can maintain creative tension by shifting from a *yes/but* structure to a *yes/and* structure. For example, "I want to eat more ecologically *and* I don't know how, *yet*." Because "and" is a joining word, it allows you to hold the two different ideas in dynamic tension. The natural tendency is to figure out an appropriate way to close the gap between them. "I want to write, *but* I have no talent" pits vision against a distorted assessment of reality. The vision is "I want to write." (Of course, vision should be clearer if it is to have power.) "But I have no talent," is a judgment. It distorts reality by absolutizing. First, it uses the verb "to be" in the form "I have." Second, the "no," implies that you never will have talent. Both rob you of optimism and hope.

It would be better to say something like, "I'm afraid my talent isn't sufficient, yet" or "My writing experience is limited to letters to friends and C-minus high school book reviews." These statements are more objective. You gain power by describing reality, rather than judging it.

Once you have vision and current reality clear, hold them in mind together, and take action to bridge the gap between where you are and where you want to be. Take a writing workshop, do daily practice sessions, or take part in an on-line workshop as first steps. The point is to separate vision and reality, generate creative tension, and get it working for you. Paying attention to the difference between "and" and "but" can help you keep yourself clear about what is vision and what is current reality. *I want to write,* but *I have no talent,* becomes *I want to write* and *I'm afraid my talent might not be enough. I want to eat more ecologically,* but *I don't know how,* becomes *I want to eat more ecologically* and *I don't know how,* **yet**.

Paying attention to the difference between "but" and "and" can be particularly useful in conversations and co-creating. I have a friend who hotly debated issues with others. Although he'd practiced active listening skills and tried to paraphrase what he heard, my friend prefaced most of his responses with "but." It sounded something like, "I understand that you think this or that, *BUT*...." He'd then share his point of view. Another friend took him aside and told him that his style of responding irritated or even hurt his conversational partners. "When you reply like that," he said, "it sounds phony. Manipulative. Even though you paraphrase the other person's point and act like you're listening, when you "but" in, it sounds as if you believe that everything before the "but" is BS. Why don't you try substituting 'and' for 'but.' It's more inclusive."

My friend took that advice. He has been a pleasure to bounce ideas around with ever since.

Tight Framework; Open Process

"But," I'm often asked by new clients, "what if I don't know *how* to do what I want?"

This is a variation on the "Yeah, but..." syndrome. It indicates a need to be clear about *how to* create a result before they start creating it. Clients fear that, because they don't know how to create the result now, they will never know how to create it. So, they put off taking action until they are clear. Waiting for clarity to come to them, some never get around to creating.

Sometimes, the only way to get clear is to do it; figure out the process as you go. That you have not done something should not deter you from starting. Creating is learning. Watch wildlife artists when they begin a project. They do preliminary studies. They sketch details of the bird or animal they want to paint. They experiment with colours and tones. As well as a way of building momentum, sketching is a way of teaching themselves how to draw and paint their subject.

Having the security of a tightly focussed, firmly grounded framework in place allows you to be open with process. Leaving the "how to" process open leaves room for learning and growth. It allows you to tap into intuition as well as your rational powers. It also allows for "free play" between rationality and intuition and adds to your creative power.

The Problem with Perfection

Perfectionism is another barrier to getting started. Some would-be creators find that they can't get started because they refuse to make mistakes. This kind of perfectionism is a curse. It prevents learning, growth, and change. It keeps you rooted where you are, held in place by fear and inertia. This kind of perfectionism usually arises out of a perception that actions are *performances* to be judged, rather than *experiments* to learn from.

It also comes from the ideal that one *must* perform perfectly at all times. Albert Ellis, the father of Rational Emotive Therapy (a precursor to cognitive behavioural therapy) stated that such "musturbating" was one of the main causes not only of inaction, but also of anxiety and depression. He advised against musturbating, especially in public. He said it was as bad or worse than "shoulding" on yourself and others. (Sorry, but the puns are just too appropriate.)

If you are afflicted by perfectionism, you likely think anything less than a *complete and successful* action is unsatisfactory. Rather than take a step-by-step, create-and-adjust approach, you focus only on vision, demanding that you achieve it perfectly. However, you are also likely to be discouraged by a less than perfect performance. Even the thought of such performances can put you off. Therefore, you don't act. You do not produce the results you want.

The Road to Great Always Runs through Better

Most procrastination arises from an idealistic perfectionism, the fear of a less-than-perfect performance. One client came to me because she wanted to be a "great" guitar player. Nothing less would satisfy her. However, she couldn't face the failure she knew she'd experience if she actually tried to play. Then she met a man she liked who played in a country-folk band. He showed her how to play a folk song using three simple chords. With a little practice and gentle coaching, she learned to play the song and sing along. That confused her. She could play a song on the guitar, but she wasn't good, let alone great. What was she? She thought about it for a while then said, "I'm better! I was a bad guitar player (in my mind) and now I'm better." From then on, she resolved to stop criticizing herself for not being good and to focus on getting better.

Although I recommended that she not use "better" to describe end results, my client's point is a good one. The road from where you are to where you want to be always runs through "better." Becoming successful is a step-by-step process. If you try to make an all or nothing leap, you might end up with nothing. You rarely learn without mistakes and setbacks. If you define mistakes as "failure," you'll stop yourself in your tracks. If you define them as feedback, opportunities to learn, and steps toward progress, you can, with patience, perseverance, and practice, produce the results you want. In the creative process, there is no failure, only feedback!

GETTING STARTED

Although getting started can be the hardest part of the creative process, once started, the process flows surprisingly well. There are numerous ways to get started and to keep moving.

Bird by Bird

Ann Lamott, writing teacher and author of the best-selling book, *Bird By Bird: Some Instructions on Writing and Life,* says that the two single most helpful things she tells beginning writers are, "Give yourself short assignments," and, "Write shitty first drafts."[49]

Lamott recommends breaking up larger challenges into bite-sized pieces. Focus on a paragraph, she suggests, not a whole piece. She illustrates her point with a story about her older brother who had a school report due on birds. He'd had three months to write it, but left it until the last night. "We were at our family cabin in Bolinas," Lamott relates, "and he was at the kitchen table close to tears, surrounded by binder paper and pencils and unopened books on birds, immobilized by the hugeness of the task ahead. Then my father sat down beside him, put his arm around my brother's shoulder, and said, "Bird by bird, buddy. Just take it bird by bird."

Creators know the importance of small steps. They know they lead to small successes. They know that patterns of success generate confidence and the energy needed to stretch for larger steps. They deliberately take small steps to create *patterns* of success. Painters sketch. Musicians work out short passages before writing them into a symphony. Authors rough out character sketches on the backs of envelopes. Sketches and drafts get you past perfectionism. They loosen you up, get the juices flowing. First steps get you started and lead to second, third,

...whatever number of drafts it takes to complete the creation. Although a draft may be far from perfect, it gets you moving.

Taking a first step is a strategic action in the creative process. It overcomes inertia and gets momentum working for you. Inertia can be intimidating, that first step the most difficult. This is because naive creators often start with steps that are too difficult, too complex, or for which they are not prepared. The key to getting started is to find simple, easy first steps, and do them.

First Steps

How do you determine your first steps? I use two ways. First, we saw how telescoping end results can work back to smaller and more doable action steps. That's one way to establish first steps. Another way of working backward to determine what must be done is the "backward planning" technique outlined by Barbara Sher in her book, *WishCraft*.[50]

Start with your vision. Look at the result you want to create and ask yourself, "Can I do this today?" If you cannot do it now, ask yourself, "What must I do first?"

If your goal is "A simple, nutritious, and ecologically healthy eating approach: a way of eating that contributes to the health of the planet as well as myself," you obviously cannot do it all today.

So what must you do first? *Change my eating patterns.*

Can you do that today? *No.* What must you do first? *Have the proper foods in my house.*

Can you do that today? *No.* What must you do first? *Choose an eating plan for myself.*

Can you do that today? *No.* What must you do first? *Gather information about eating plans.*

Can you do that today? *Not completely.* What must you do first? *Find where such information is located.*

Can you do that today? *No.* What do you have to do first? *Call the Ecology Centre or the public library to see if they have such information. Or surf the Net to see if I can find it there.*

Can you do that now? *No, I don't have the numbers or the URLs.*

What do you have to do first? *Look up the numbers in the phone book. Or a computer search.*

Can you do that now? *Yes!* Then there's your first step. *Do it!*

Breaking results into small, doable tasks — "short assignments" — identifies the steps to get you started. Taking one step often leads to another, then another. Taking several leads to a pattern of success and momentum toward further actions. For Celia and Al, gathering information about healthy eating plans led to interest in organic gardening and eventually to them joining a cohousing group. Success leads to success. Vision grows in the doing.

Working back to first steps may seem like overkill to some. However, many of my clients' and my own efforts failed because we trivialized and overlooked small, simple things. Paul is a simple liver and a dedicated environmentalist who tries hard to walk his talk. However, he found that he was not fully able to act on some of his environmental goals until he discovered and put in place what he calls *working systems.* He wanted to use string bags to carry groceries home from the store, and to re-use small paper and plastic bags, but he'd forget. He'd show up at the store without his bags and have to use new ones. When he worked back to first steps, he realized that the key to being consistent was to make sure that his small bags were stuffed in his string bags and that the string bags were always handy and visible. So he screwed a hook into the wall beside his door and hung his bags on it. Now he rarely forgets them. They're by the door where he can see them. The simple first step of putting a hook in the wall was a strategic action that enabled Paul to consistently take the larger actions that mattered to him.

First steps are important because a powerful vision by itself can be overwhelming. Many people, for example, have visions about "saving the Earth." This is admirable, but people with such large visions often say, sometimes consciously, often unconsciously, "*I* could never do that." And they can't, not all at once. But we don't do visions. We do small steps, one at a time.

Recall the old French story about two stone masons? The masons were working side by side, when a stranger approached them and asked what they were doing. The first, scowling and muttering to himself, replied, "I take a brick from that pile and put it on this wall. Then I take another and another and so on, all day long." The second mason, whistling while he worked, obviously enjoying himself, smiled knowingly and said, "Sir, I am building a great cathedral, one that will stand for a thousand years!"

"Great deeds," says Barbara Sher in *Wishcraft*, echoing Helen Keller's insight about small tasks, "are made up of small, steady actions."

Although backward planning will sometimes give you a whole series of actions steps, much like a plan, I recommend using it as a way to identify first steps and get a rough overview of what's needed to create your result. Once started, you can let the path of least resistance emerge by being open to whatever next step occurs to you. As you take action and build patterns of success, reality will change. Some actions will move you closer to your vision; some will move you away. Continually reestablish creative tension and let the *process* emerge from within the creative container. You may choose to follow the path that you laid out in your backward planning, or you might invent a more effective way as you learn from your doing.

Always remember to consciously create patterns of success that give rise to momentum. Momentum is a powerful force that works for you even as you resolve creative tension. In the next chapter, we'll examine how to build and sustain momentum and to use it as a force with which to follow through and complete results that matter.

Chapter Thirteen

The Practice of Building Momentum

"Momentum will get you through times of no motivation better than motivation will get you through times of no momentum."

What the *Fabulous Furry Freak Brothers* might have said, had they been Coaches

Successful creators are no more willing to settle for lesser results than are perfectionists. Indeed many creators are perfectionists in that they set extremely high standards for the results they create. However, they've learned different lessons than the procrastinating perfectionists who don't even try. Creators know that if a thing is worth doing, it's worth doing until you get it right. That's what practice is about. If you don't get it right at first, keep trying. Create and adjust, create and adjust…. Even doing it wrong gets you moving. It builds momentum. Once you have momentum working for you, it's easier to make adjustments and change directions. The best way to build momentum is to practice, practice, practice.

The Power of Practice

Practice is pivotal in the creative process. Through practice, the mind, body, and spirit come together in a synergy of mastery. Practice sharpens skills, increases flexibility and power, and leads to deeper understanding. Practice builds competence, which gives you confidence to stretch and grow. Practice helps you persist with awkward techniques that must be done slowly and deliberately until mastered. Then they become automatic; you do them with ease and grace. Mastery allows you to enter the flow state that arises when your level of competence is appropriate to the challenge you face.

In my *Simplicity and Success* workshops and retreats, I can tell by the second session who will produce results and who will struggle. Those who do the assigned practice between sessions almost always go on to produce outstanding results. Those who don't practice rarely produce results. When I ask them, "Why not?" they claim they didn't have time, or don't like doing homework, or that they learn better in their heads. I ask them, "If you wanted to learn to ski or play the piano, would you just go to lectures and read books?" *No*, they say. "How would you learn those things," I ask. *Practice*, they grudgingly reply. "Well?" I ask.

Many suffer from what I call "the academic fallacy," the mistaken belief that knowing *about* something is the same as knowing how to do it. It isn't. Mastery requires that we integrate understanding and experience. It is a tragic oversight that our educational system values "knowing about" at the expense of integrated "thinking and doing." I think this is one reason why we have become consumers rather than creators. Social reformer Ivan Illich claims schools turn young people into consumers by teaching "the need to be taught." Much of the powerlessness that feeds the insatiable drive for relief products may stem from learning the lessons of schooling all too well.

Creating is a form of mastery. It integrates understanding and experience. In it, the head, heart, and hands come together to give rise to the most powerful technique for producing results ever invented. In the creative process, thinking, feeling, and doing are *all* essential. At the end of my courses, those who practice, who engage their heart and hands as well as their heads often say that doing the course changed their life. Those who don't practice say things like, "It was interesting, but it didn't do much for me." That's probably because they didn't *do* much.

The dictionary defines skill as "practiced ability." In *Free Play*, Stephen Nachmanovitch says, "Not only is practice necessary to art, it *is* art." Creators don't see practice as homework. They see it as a way of life. Their art is their practice; their practice is their art. Writing teacher Colleen Rae poetically underscores the power of practice in her book *Movies of the Mind*. Through practice, she says, creators develop artful ways to "pull the new into the now."[51]

Practice may not make you perfect, but it does allow you to learn from your mistakes and to stay on the learning curve until you can create with ease and elegance.

Staying On the Curve

The concept of "learning curve" is a useful way to show how practice and experience accumulate into successful results. Unfortunately, many people do not understand learning curve dynamics. For example, I often hear some people complain that they're on a steep learning curve when they are actually on the flat part of the curve. On the learning curve, "steep" means accelerating returns, exponential increases in learning, and a high ratio of results to effort. People confuse steep with difficult and miss the most important lessons of the learning curve.

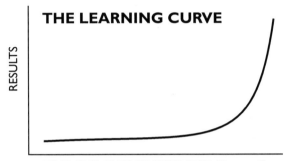

In the beginning of any learning or creating project, learning is slow. You put in large amounts of time and energy without generating significant results. If you continue to practice, your skill and competence increase until, at the far right of the curve, small amounts of time and energy generate rapid, even spectacular, increases in results. On learning curves, steep is good!

Extensive research shows that learning of all kinds unfolds according to Parreto's Law (or the 80/20 principle). Parreto's Law states that the last twenty percent of your effort produces eighty percent of your results. Therefore, the key to those results is to stay on the curve until it steepens and mastery emerges. Filmmaker Woody Allen captured the essence of this dynamic when he quipped, "Eight-five percent of success comes from just showing up each day."

Creators understand showing up every day. Writers go to their room and write every day. Painters and sculptors go to their studios. They *do* their creating. Although it can be a struggle, particularly when they take on new projects, they know to stay on the curve until they experience the exhilarating rise in learning and skill that comes from the last twenty percent of their effort. They also know that it's the first eighty percent of effort that makes the last twenty possible. The key to making it to the steep part of the learning curve is getting started and keeping moving.

Building Momentum

Momentum keeps you moving even as creative tension is resolved and loses its power. Momentum carries you through to the completion of creations.

The most important time to keep momentum up is when you experience difficulties and setbacks and are tempted to quit. If you make a mistake or suffer a setback, the tension in the framework increases, making it more likely that your next action will move you in the direction you want to go. So after a setback, simply re-establish creative tension by clarifying your vision, checking current reality, and choosing the result you want. Then move on to your next action.

Moving on might mean repeating the previous action. Or making a slight adjustment and then trying it again. If you're stuck, it might mean improvising or "messing around," playing with ideas or actions to see what emerges. You might have to step back, take a different view, and come at it from a different angle. Or, perhaps, do more research or develop new or more sophisticated skills.

There are two main ways to keep momentum working for you. First, keep taking action. It's easier to change direction and correct mistakes when you're moving than when you lose momentum and have to start from a dead stop. To keep moving, always know what your next step is going to be, or your next couple of steps. You might get materials in place for the next phase of your creation, even as you're working on the current stage. This way, when you finish one stage of a project, you're ready to move on to the next without a loss of momentum.

The second way to maintain momentum is to make sure you assess reality objectively and accurately. Following setbacks, errors and failures, many people judge the situation and themselves. Judgments are often negative and absolute. "I'm a failure. I'm a klutz. There's no point in continuing this." Such judgments destroy momentum. On the other hand, the "yet" lesson the rock climbing executives learned builds momentum. When you feel stymied by difficulty, setbacks, or an inability to do what you want, add the word "yet" to your description of the situation. I can't do this, *yet*. I don't know where to get the money, *yet*. Adding "yet" opens you up to possibilities and secondary choices that you may not have considered.

And Now For Something Completely Different

One of the most important momentum building techniques is the *Creative Moment* technique you learned in Chapter Eight. That technique ends with the suggestion to "Move on." Moving on is not necessarily linear. Sometimes, when faced with failure or a setback, the best thing to do is something completely different. Move to another task. Go for a walk, take a shower, change the subject, read a novel, juggle, write a letter to a friend, cast the *I Ching*. Give your rational mind a rest, surrender a little, and let your intuition work on your creation. Let next steps emerge organically as you shift your focus. Countless stories tell of scientists who, faced with dead ends, turned to other activities. No longer focussed directly on a result they sought, they suddenly perceived new ways to approach it. Kekulé envisioned the structure of benzene while dozing in front of his fire after dinner. Pascal made a major mathematical discovery as he stepped onto a bus on his way to the seashore. Archimedes had his famous "Eureka!" experience in the bathtub.

My favourite technique for moving on when I get stuck writing is to go outside and juggle for ten or fifteen minutes. Juggling gets me out of my head. It gets my hands and eyes working together. It engrosses me. Sometimes I slip into flow. After a short while, I go back inside and sit down at my computer and it's like I was never stuck at all. I taught this technique to Celia and Al. They loved it. "It's so simple," said Celia, but so powerful."

Rather than let setbacks set you back, learn to use them. There is no failure in the creative process, only feedback. Remember what the artist, Nicoliades, said in *The Natural Way to Draw*: "The sooner you make your first 5000 mistakes, the sooner you will learn to draw."[52] In the creative framework, every result you produce provides useful information about the effectiveness of your actions. Feeding back information about partial or failed results into the framework changes your assessment of current reality and gives rise to new actions.

Adjust any actions that do not produce results you want. Amplify actions that do produce results. Building on success with new and bolder actions enables you to stretch. Within the creative framework, everything you do can work in your favour. To ensure you remain within that framework, even in difficult circumstances, do the following:

1. Be conscious of the actions you take and the results they produce.
2. Carefully describe current reality. Don't judge it.
3. Recreate creative tension by asking, "What do I want?" and "What do I have?"
4. Take actions that keep you moving toward your vision.
5. Repeat the process with each action you take.

Create and adjust, create and adjust.... Take action, evaluate results, correct mistakes. Step by step, or as my Mexican friends say, *"poco a poco"* — little by little — you move toward final results guided by the structure and tension of the creative framework.

The Power of Momentum: A Fifteen Minute Test

Like any coach, I sometimes (okay, often) have trouble taking my own advice. I sometimes find it challenging to practice what I preach. But when I do, I produce results like those I describe in the following anecdote. I wrote this section one morning while trying to write a different piece and couldn't get started. This is what I came up with.

Thanksgiving morning. A good time to write. No interruptions. No calls. I'm alone. The house is quiet. I have no plans. Nothing to do but write. "But," I hear an inner voice whine, "I don't feel like writing. I'm tired. It's a holiday. I shouldn't have to work. I need a rest."

I'm confused. My head says I want to write; but the rest of me says it's not a good time. I'm not in the mood. I have nothing to say. I don't *feel* like writing. I'm in a lull. I pushed hard to finish two stories for a contest. Now I'm coasting. I've got an article that needs revising, but I want to write something new, not revise. *Just write*, I tell myself, *put words on paper*. But my self doesn't want to waste time putting words on paper. I make myself a pot of tea and flip on the TV.

A talk show about aliens reminds me of Ray Bradbury, the great science fiction writer, and the advice he gave would-be writers in *Zen In the Art of Writing*. If you want be a writer, he said, first "write a million words."[53] I switch off the TV and ponder this advice. Putting words on paper, even bad words, will, I know, bring me closer to my first million. It will bring me closer to being the writer I want to be. Quality will come, I reason, with time. For now, work on quantity; put words on paper. I go back to my desk and start writing. But it doesn't work. Halfway through the first paragraph, I quit. It *feels* awful. "This is crap," sneers my Voice of Judgment. "You *should* be able to write better than this." I get up from my chair. I can't face my obvious limitations. Suddenly, I discover an abundance of excuses not to write. My wrist aches, so do my forearms. The voice says, "Ah! Carpel tunnel syndrome. Why not read a book on writing ? Maybe you need inspiration before you can write." Or maybe, I think, I need a diversion. Maybe I should go for a walk and reflect on nature. There might be a piece in that. Or I could hang out at the Café and make notes on people. No. Too much like writing. I feel like going down to the pub for a beer, but it's only 9 AM. Frustrated, I begin to pace the hallway outside my office.

Before I learned to do my *Fifteen Minute Test*, I would give into my feelings and quit. But now I do a fifteen-minute experiment. I choose to write without stopping for fifteen minutes, even if it's only about not wanting to write. And this simple test makes a huge difference in my results. I use this technique to overcome the depressing, down moods that used to sabotage my good intentions and get in the way of creating results, not only in writing, but in all areas of my life. I came by this momentum-building technique from two disparate sources: from my experience as a road-runner, and from a quote about "mood" from the writer Joyce Carol Oates.

In an interview in *The Paris Review*, Oates said,

> One must be pitiless about this matter of 'mood.' In a sense the writing will create the mood. ... Generally I have found this to be true: I have forced myself to begin writing when I've been utterly exhausted, when I've felt

my soul as thin as a playing card, when nothing has seemed worth enduring for another five minutes ... and somehow the activity of writing changes everything.[54]

As an aspiring road-runner, I often faced the "I want to, but don't feel like it," dilemma. I'd come home from work feeling frustrated and fatigued. I'd say to my wife, "I'm too tired to run today. I'm going to put my feet up and have a Scotch."

"Go for a run, honey," she'd say. "It always makes you feel better." I knew she was right, but the prospect of pounding hard pavement for ten or more miles seemed overwhelming. "There's no way!" I'd say to myself. "I couldn't run two miles tonight, so what's the point?" I'd work myself into an all-or-nothing conundrum. Run the whole distance, or stay home and drink Scotch. The Scotch often won out. It was easy, convenient, and immediately pleasurable. When I *really* didn't feel like running, I could trump any pro-running argument my wife might put forward by playing my Ace of Health. "I feel like I might be coming down with something," I'd whine. "Maybe I should stay home, rest up, and perhaps have a wee dram or two for medicinal purposes."

One night, having just played that ace, I was taking the bottle of single malt down from the kitchen cupboard when a new voice in my head said, "Why don't you check it out?"

"What?" I replied. "Check out what? How?"

"Check out whether you really are fatigued," said this calm, reasonable sounding voice. "Maybe your blood sugar's low. Perhaps you're just being lazy. Why don't you do a little test? Try running for fifteen minutes. See if the activity changes anything."

"Fifteen minutes?" I said.

"Yes," said the voice, "that's how long it'll take for your blood sugar to come up to normal. Then you'll feel better. If you don't, perhaps there *is* something wrong. If so, quit, walk home, and have a drink without guilt. See it as an experiment."

I fingered the cap on the Scotch bottle, mulling over this strange but seemingly reasonable thought. "What could it hurt?" I thought. "It's only fifteen minutes."

I left the Scotch out on the counter then went downstairs to change. I stretched easily, then slipped into my rain suit. Outside, I began a slow lumbering jog. The early autumn air was cool and damp. Heavy clouds massed in treetops. My muscles ached. I had no energy. Each step jarred my head. *This,* I thought, turning into the park, *is a mistake.* I laboured around the cinder path, scanning my body for signs of illness, for an excuse to quit. Instead I relaxed into the run. After fifteen minutes, I felt a surge of energy. Momentum built with each step. My muscles loosened as tension melted like butter under a hot sun. The cares of the day fell away. I stretched out my stride and picked up my pace. *I'll go another fifteen minutes,* I said, *see how it goes.*

I didn't check my watch again for over an hour. I ran down to the river and along the path that winds along the bank. I ran all the way to the footbridge, crossed the river, and scampered through the old Douglas fir forest. Then I dropped back down to the river path and ran hard all the way to the island. I jogged easily around the island, smiling at other runners and seniors with small dogs. I giggled to myself as I walked home. I'd just run twelve miles! And felt great.

I'd also taught myself a valuable lesson that I could apply to life and work. Now, whenever I don't *feel* like doing what I *want* to do, I do a "Fifteen Minute Test." It works for writing, yard work, even doing tax returns. I try it for fifteen minutes to see if my mood shifts, if momentum leads to motivation. If it doesn't, I try another fifteen minutes, or give it up and do something else. Nine out of ten times I keep going. The activity changes everything. Often I surprise myself with results like the twelve-mile run. On the rare occasions when I do stop, I feel no guilt or remorse. I know it's right to quit. And because of that, the Scotch tastes so much better.

Oh yeah, about Thanksgiving morning? It took me less than an hour to write the first draft of this section. Then I switched to the project that had stumped me. The momentum I'd produced with this piece fueled a full, productive and satisfying day of writing. It also got me a couple of thousand words closer to my first million words.

Chapter Fourteen

Commitment and Completion

Until one is committed there is hesitancy, the chance to draw back, always ineffectiveness. Concerning all acts of initiative (and creation), there is one elementary truth, the ignorance of which kills countless ideas and splendid plans: that the moment one definitely commits oneself, then Providence moves too.

W.H. Murray

Commitment is critical in creating. It's a catalyzing step in the creative process. It sparks energy and keeps the flame of passion alive. It also scares many people. "Where do you get the discipline to force yourself to write?" friends and clients ask me. "How do you commit to such large projects when you have no idea if they'll be successful?"

Commitment to results that matter does *not* come from forcing yourself. It arises out of the clarity of your vision, and from the fact that you'd love to create that result and give it to the world. Recall that Stephen Nachmanovitch said the word "*desire*" comes from *de-sidere,* 'away from your star.'" When you care *deeply* about a result and ground your vision in current reality, an almost irresistible attraction pulls you toward that result. Forced discipline does not get Olympic athletes up at 4:00 AM to train. Nor does willpower or self-manipulation through fear or guilt. Great athletes are motivated by clear visions of results they want to create.

A Canadian Olympic swimmer once shared with me his secret for dealing with the doubts and uncertainty that sometimes afflicted him. "Whenever I feel my commitment flagging," he said, "and feel like I just can't swim another length of the pool, I take a few moments to myself. I sit down, take a few deep breaths, close my eyes, and envision myself on the top step of the podium with a gold medal around my neck. I hear "Oh, Canada" being played. I feel myself fighting back tears while our flag is raised. And when I look down, I see an American on one side of me and an Australian on the other. They smile and reach up to shake my hand."

"Wow!" I said, "That's a powerful vision."

"There's more," he said. "I savour my vision for a few moments. Then I compare it to where I am, to my best times to date. When I clearly see the difference between where I am and where I want to be, it's easy to choose to get back in the pool and swim my heart out."

Without vision grounded in reality, all the discipline, willpower, and self-trickery in the world will not sustain athletes in their quest for results. It is the same for all creators. To be committed there must be something worth committing to, something that you care deeply about creating.

The Importance of Completion

You need commitment to get started. You also need it to follow through to completed results. Commitment may not always lead to success, but it does lead to completion. Creators understand the importance of completing creations. Completing is about finishing fully, pulling together the pieces of a creation into a final form, which you judge as complete. Completion allows you to let go. It generates a surge of energy you can use to start on your next creation. If painters refused to judge their paintings as complete, they would never put them out into the world, nor move on to new paintings with renewed energy and vitality. Writers who insist on endlessly polishing a story before they submit it rarely progress beyond that unfinished story.

There comes a time in the creative process when the creator says "Good enough. What's out there looks close enough to what I have always envisioned in my mind. It's done." The painting is signed. The manuscript is sent to the publisher.

A woman in one of my workshops told us that as a teenager she'd learned to knit from her mother who was a master knitter. She developed a high degree of skill and finesse in the basics of knitting, but always deferred to her mother when it came time to sew the pieces of a project together. Later, living by herself, she decided to knit a sweater. She worked for weeks and completed all the pieces. Then she realized she didn't now how to sew the arms to the body. She put the sweater in a drawer and left it there for twenty years. She did not knit another stitch on it — or on any other project. During the workshop, she decided to learn to sew her pieces and complete her sweater as one of her creating practices. The next week she came to class wearing the most beautiful Irish cable knit sweater I'd seen. It had been a wonderful week, she reported. As soon as she finished her sweater, she'd started knitting sweaters for her kids. She loved her renewed commitment to the craft she'd abandoned.

Completing a creation is sometimes difficult because you do not want it to end. It's like being wrapped up in a compelling and entertaining novel. You're so involved in it, you don't want it to end. A sense of satisfaction and a sense of sadness can accompany completion. Actors in a long-running play are glad to be finished, yet sad the play is over. Sailors returning from a long journey have the same mix of emotions. Because they experience sadness on completion, some would-be creators are reluctant to bring their creations to fruition. They prefer the process to the result. But in the creative process, the result does matter. The desire for the result is what gives rise to the process. You must be willing to let go of the process and the good feelings that come with creating if you are to complete and give your creation to the world.

Other creators rev up as they close in on completion. They get so excited that they speed up the project. They push it toward completion faster than it wants to proceed. As they do, their focus narrows, sometimes to the point where they miss important information. Setbacks occur, problems pop up. All because the creator gets over-anxious and careless. You can't hold on to a creation too long and you can't push a creation to completion before its time. Part of the art of creating is to know when you're done and then let go gracefully.

Accepting and Acknowledging

Completion has two parts: *acknowledging* and *accepting*. You need to acknowledge your results, to judge them "good enough" in the light of your vision. Moreover, you need to accept your results, to affirm your success, to shake off your failures, and let yourself enjoy the fruits of your labor. Once you produce a result, your relationship with it shifts from creator to critic. When you are in the process of creating, you abstain from judgment in favour of objectively describing current reality. However, there is a time when judgment plays an important part in the creative process. You acknowledge that your creation is complete. You judge that it matches your vision, or is close enough. At this point, the creation takes on a life of its own, separate from you. You stand in judgment of it, like any other observer. In addition, whether it's good or bad, you accept the creation and live with it, knowing it is separate from you.

Many people do not let themselves *accept* the results of their efforts. You can see this by how they respond when they are complimented. They will put off a compliment by saying "it was nothing," or "I was just lucky." They give credit to someone else. Some downplay their results: "It's just a piece of junk I threw together." By not accepting the results they have created, these individuals fail to affirm their efforts. They do not complete the creative process. They do not experience the energy and momentum that comes with completion. Here, affirmation is critical. Affirming success generates the energy and confidence needed to stretch for your next creation.

Creators sometimes produce results they do not like. So be it. If you don't like a creation, create something else. Every creator has experienced making a piece that was exactly what was envisioned yet did not please that creator. Rather than be upset by the piece, accomplished creators use the experience of making it — and the learning they gained — as the foundation for their next piece. John Fowles was not happy with his best-selling novel, *The Magus*. Twenty years later, armed with experience and mastery, he re-wrote it. Pablo Picasso was once asked which was his favourite painting. He quickly replied, "My next one."

Sharing Your Light

One of the things that distinguishes a creator from the dabbler is the willingness to put creations out into the world and to live with them — regardless of what other people, or even the creator, thinks of the final product. Many people fail to create what they truly want because they fear what others might say about it, or them. They hide their ideas and visions away. They invest their life energy in things that are not as important as their deepest dreams and desires. They compromise. They do what they want second most, rather than what they *truly* want.

Some settle for less than what they truly want because they don't want to look arrogant or pushy. I've had people ask me, "Who are you to be writing and teaching about this stuff?" My answer is that experience has taught me that people find what I write and teach useful. Plus, I love it. For whatever reason though, many people go through life without ever attempting to realize their highest aspirations or deepest longings. This is a loss to all of us. I advise those who fear failing at what matters to step up and take their best swing, to feel the fear and do it anyway.

"But," they ask, "what if I fail?" People who ask this question rarely answer it consciously. Instead, they fantasize about negative circumstances flowing from their "failure." They imagine failure as absolute, unchanging, and devastating. It terrifies them. "Really think about the question," I suggest. "What would you do if you failed at something you truly wanted?"

Most think about this for a moment, then say, "I guess if I truly wanted it, I'd try again. I'd figure out a way to do it." I remind them of authors such as Robert Pirsig, whose novel *Zen and the Art of Motorcycle Maintenance* was rejected by over 100 publishers before it became a best seller. "What," I ask, "if Pirsig had defined a dozen rejections as 'failure?'" If a thing is worth doing, it is worth doing again and again — until you get it right.

The philosopher Thomas Aquinas said that when you avoid creating because you don't want to look arrogant, you withdraw from your power. Failing to take a stand for your greatness is worse than arrogance. In *Creation Spirituality*, Matthew Fox says, "Aquinas feels that pusillanimity — the burying of your talents — is a greater sin than presumption, since thereby a person withdraws from good things. There is more danger in your remaining small and thus depriving others of your gifts than in offering those gifts and thus tempting pride, ambition or envy."[55]

Learn to acknowledge and accept the creations you create, then live with them. Let them take on a life of their own. Doing so enables you to come in to your own power. It empowers you to give your gifts freely to your community and the world. Anything less and you're not being true to the self you "glimpse," as Abraham Maslow put it, "in your most perfect moments."

The Day to Day Practice of Creating

Every day affords you an opportunity to practice creating. While you may not always create a masterpiece, you can create with mastery. Instead of viewing your days and your life as a series of problems to solve or struggles to overcome, view each day and each aspect of that day as a creation to bring into being — your gift to the world. Create actual creations that you want to give to the world. In addition, live your life within the creative orientation, flowing in the creative process. Here are a few hints for creating days that are filled with creative flow.

Each day, make foundation choices. Choose to be free. Choose to be healthy. Choose to be true to yourself. Choose to be the predominant creative force in your life. Make other foundation choices that are basic to the life you want to create. I choose to live a simple yet rich, focussed, and sustainable life in harmony with the systems that sustain all life. I also choose to be successful at what matters to me in a way that matters to the world. Make the choices that work for you.

Each morning and evening, practice holding creative tension for five minutes. Choose one result and hold a clear vision of it in tension with current reality. Be gentle; don't force it. Just hold the images in mind together and allow yourself to feel the tension that arises out of the gap between them. Then choose what you want to create.

Notice when you're uptight, frustrated, or depressed. Emotional tension tells you that you're in problem-solving. See that as part of current reality; set up a creative framework and generate creative tension by focussing on what you want. Commit to your vision; choose it. Hold it in tension with current reality. Describe current reality objectively; let go of judgments about reality. Remember to practice the *Creative Moment* technique. It puts you back into creating. Watch your self-talk. Monitor what you say and how you say it. Notice if you're exaggerating aspects of current reality. Notice if you're judging what you see rather than describing it. Don't absolutize. Don't should on yourself and others. If you catch yourself telling a victim story, tell yourself a creator's story. Self-talk is the key to current reality and to a healthy life.

Chart out your creations, at least at first. Make a master, first level chart for each major creation. Telescope the action steps into second and third level charts. Learn to envision the fractal nature of creating and to see that even the smallest steps are connected directly to the largest results. Above all, practice holding creative tension, taking action, and learning as you go. Practice every day, stay on the curve, and let the power of learning accelerate your results.

Creating, I hope you can now see, is not some magic gift from the gods granted only to a few. Creating is a complex mix of form, skill, and practice. To master the skills and form of creating, make it a daily "practice," as martial artists, meditators, and musicians do.

This book provides only a sketchy map of some of the territory. There is far more to the creative process than has been described here. Your task is to use the map to explore your own life, your own work, your own creative process. Your challenge is to use the skills and framework to create what matters most to you. Above all, it's to live your life as a creator.

Endings Are Also Beginnings

In "The Four Quartets," poet T.S. Eliot, said, "We shall not cease from exploration, and the end of all our exploring will be to arrive where we started, and know that place for the first time."

We've come a long way since Celia's first phone call when she asked how she and Al could solve problems and get rid of complexity. It wasn't easy for this couple to learn to create, but they did. After they'd taken several workshops with me, they continued their coaching sessions, alone and together. They clarified what mattered to each of them and as a couple. They moved from an apartment into an urban co-housing complex that they helped develop. They both took four-day-a week jobs with an Urban Sustainability Institute. Celia teaches *creating* to others in the co-housing group and in the surrounding neighbourhood. Their relationship is stronger, richer, and more flexible. Each feels like more of an individual *and* more connected to the other.

"Since we learned to create," said Celia, "our lives have become much simpler and more successful in all the ways that count. My life feels integrated now, like the pieces and parts align with all the other pieces and parts. I love it."

"Although I was skeptical that anyone could learn to create," Al said, "I stuck with it and I'm glad I did. Our lives have gone from scattered, frustrating messes to relaxed, flowing examples of the creative process in action. I'm very grateful for what I've learned and what I've been able to create. I developed gifts I never knew I had and am able to give those gifts to others. There's no feeling like doing that successfully. And it's so simple, once you know how."

Celia and Al, along with Sarah, Murray, Sandra, Sharon and Don, Dave and Beth and all the others who shared their stories with us in this book mastered the skills and framework of creating and applied it to creating the life, work, and world they most wanted. The results they produced are unique to each of them, but all of them achieved two results they had in common. They integrated simplicity and success and created a life and work that, as Thomas Merton urged, expressed their highest and most enduring values. Their visions became realities. Mostly, they tell me, they all found their way to the real and lasting simplicity on the other side of complexity.

Through my own exploration, I too have arrived at where I began and know that place for the first time. This book now looks on paper like it's always looked in my head. Thanks for sticking with me on this journey. I wish you the very best in *your* life as a creator.

Let's give the last word to the Hebrew scholar Hillel, who asked:

> *If not for yourself, who will be?*
> *But, if for yourself alone, then who are you?*
> *If not now, when?*

Bruce Elkin,
Saltspring Island, BC

About the Author

Bruce Elkin has lived simply and successfully for twenty five years. He is a Personal, Professional, and Executive Coach and President of *Summit Strategies,* a Strategic Design and Planning firm. He has taught his *Simplicity and Success* approach to clients as diverse as single moms on welfare to Fortune 500 executives. He taught at Simon Fraser University, the University of Calgary, and the Banff Centre. For five years, he was Senior Trainer for *The Institute for Earth Education.* He was a founding Associate of the *Action Studies Institute.* For nine years, he studied and worked with Robert Fritz, author of *The Path of Least Resistance* and founder of the field of *Structural Consulting.* Bruce writes and publishes *Simplicity and Success*, a popular electronic newsletter. His firm but caring coaching and enthusiastic teaching and talks have helped thousands discover what they love and live a life that shows it.

Workshops, Retreats, and Coaching Opportunities

If you would like information about Bruce's *Simplicity and Success* workshops, retreats, and coaching approach, contact him at:

141 Seaview Road
Saltspring Island, BC
V8K 2V8
Telephone: 250-537-1177
E-mail: belkin@saltspring.com

To subscribe to the *Simplicity and Success* e-newsletter, and for updates on workshops, training, and coaching opportunities, please visit Bruce's website at www.BruceElkin.com or www.SimplicityandSuccess.com

NOTES

1 "Voluntary Simplicity (3)" by Duane Elgin and Arnold Mitchell, *The Co-Evolution Quarterly*, Summer 1977

2 The original version of *The Path of Least Resistance* was revised, expanded and published as *The Path of Least Resistance: Learning to become the Creative Force in Your Own Life*, Fawcett Columbine, New York [1989] Fritz also wrote *The Path of Least Resistance for Managers: Desiging organizations to Succeed*, Publisher's Group West [1999].

3 Fritz's principles are not trendy, here-today-gone-tomorrow ideas. He has taught these principles for twenty-five years. They are applicable to all areas of life and living. Peter Senge, director of Organizational Learning and Systems Thinking at MIT's Sloan School of Business, and author of the best-selling business book, *The Fifth Discipline*, says, "The principles and approach presented in *The Path of Least Resistance* have become a cornerstone in my work to help leaders and managers deal productively with complexity and change." (In *TFC, Inc.'s* promotional material.)

4 In Robert Fritz, *The Path of Least Resistance* (Fawcett Columbine) New York, 1989

5 The names and descriptions of most clients have been altered to ensure confidentiality.

6 Juliet B. Schor, *The Overspent American: Upscaling, Downshifting, and the New Consumer*, Basic Books [1998]

7 Stephen Nachmanovitch, *Free Play, Improvisation in Life and Art*, Jeremy Tarcher, Los Angeles [1990]

8 Michael Phillips, The Seven Laws of Money, Shambala Publications, Boston [1974]

9 Edward de Bono, *Simplicity*, Viking [1998]

10 In "Voluntary Simplicity," by Richard Gregg, *Co-Evolution Quarterly*, Summer 1977

11 Joe Dominguez and Vicki Robin, *Your Money Or Your Life*, Penguin Books, New York [1992]

12 Donella Meadows, "Dancing With Systems," *Whole Earth*, Winter 20001

13 Margaret Wheately and Myron Kellner-Rogers, *"A Simpler Way,"* Berrett-Koehler, San Francisco (1996)

14 Ken Wilber, *A Theory of Everything: An Integral Vision for Business, Politics, Science, and Spirituality*, Shambala, Boston [2000]

15 Eric Fromm, *To Have or To Be?* The Continuum Publishing Co.,

New York [1997]

[16] *Stewart Brand, "Living Below Your Means,"* Co-Evolution Quarterly, Summer 1977

[17] Robert Fritz, *A Short Course In Creating What You Always Wanted To But Couldn't Because Nobody Ever Told You How Because They Didn't Know Either.* DMA, Salem, MA [1985]

[18] All the quotes in this chapter from E.F. Schumacher are out of, *A Guide for the Perplexed*, Harper and Row, New York [1977]

[19] Rainer Maria Rilke, *Letters to a Young Poet*, W.W. Norton & Company, New York [1994]

[20] Marvin Weisbord, *Discovering Common Ground* [Berrett-Koehler] San Francisco 1992

[21] Ibid.

[22] James Ogilvy, *Living Without A Goal* [Currency/Doubleday] New York, 1995

[23] For more on structural conflict, see Robert Fritz's *Path of Least Resistance* books and *Your Life As Art*, Newfane Press [2003]

[24] Draper L. Kaufman, Jr. in *Systems One: An Introduction to Systems Thinking*, Future Systems, Inc. Minneapolis

[25] Stephen Nachmanovitch, *Free Play*

[26] John Briggs, *Fire in the Crucible: The Self-Creation of Creativity and Genius*, Jeremy Tarcher, Los Angeles [1990]

[27] Robert Pirsig, *Zen and the Art of Motorcycle Maintenance*, William Morrow New York (1974)

[28] In "The Four Ways of Creativity," by Angeles Arrien, in *The Soul of Creativity*, Tona Pearce Myers, Ed., New World Library, Novato, CA [1999]

[29] *Intuition Magazine*, August 1977

[30] In Goleman, et al, *The Creative Spirit*, Plume [1993]

[31] Robert Fritz, from whom I learned this framework, calls it (and the tension inherent in it) "structural tension" because the tension is created by the structure in which the parts are arranged. Peter Senge calls both framework and tension, "creative tension." Marvin Minsky, in *The Society of Mind*, Simon and Schuster, New York [1986] uses the terms "goal driven systems," and "difference engines" to refer to frameworks that integrate a desired state and the actual state. He also says that earlier scholars such as Herbert A. Simon called such systems "general problem solvers." In spite of different terms used to describe these frameworks, there is a consensus about the impact of harnessing and directing the tension that arises out of the discrepancy between

vision and reality. "From Heraclitus to Augustine," says Thomas Berry, "to Nicholas of Cusa, Hegel and Marx, to Jung, Teilhard and Prigogine, creativity has been associated with a disequilibrium, a tension of forces."

[32] Registered Retirement Savings Plan. The Canadian equivalent to a 401(k) retirement savings account.

[33] Geoffrey Vickers, *Freedom in a Rocking Boat: Changing Values in an Unstable Society*, Penguin, GB [1970]

[34] Joe Dominguez and Vicki Robin, *Your Money Or Your Life*, Penguin Books, New York [1992]

[35] Eric Booth, *The Everyday Work of Art: How Artistic Experience Can Transform Your Life*, Sourcebooks [1997]

[36] Ben Fong-Torres, *Hickory Wind: The Life and Times of Gram Parsons*, Giffin Trade Paperback [1998]

[37] Byron Katie, *Loving What Is: Four Questions That Can Change Your Life*, Harmony Books, New York [2202]

[38] Rosamund Stone Zander and Benjamin Zander, *The Art of Possibility: Transforming Professional and Personal Life*, Harvard Business School Press, Boston, MA, [2000]

[39] Cited in Michael Maccoby, *Why Work? Leading the New Generation*, Simon and Schuster, New York [1988]

[40] Mihaly Csikszentmihalyi, *Finding Flow: The Psychology of Engagement in Everyday Life*, Basic Books, New York [1998]

[41] Peter Senge, *The Fifth Discipline: The Art and Practice of the Learning Organization*, Doubleday, New York [1990]

[42] Michael Phillips, *The Seven Laws of Money*, Shambala Publications, Boston [1974]

[43] Robert Fritz, *Creating*, Fawcett Columbine, New York [1991]

[44] From Marianne Williamson, *A Return to Love* HarperCollins, New York (1992) in *The Art of Possibility*, Rosamund Stone Zander and Benjamin Zander, Harvard Business School Press, Boston (2000)

[45] Ken Wilber, *A Theory of Everything: An Integral Vision for Business, Politics, Science, and Spirituality*, Shambala, Boston [2000]

[46] Murray, W. H., *The Story of Everest*, J.M. Dent & Sons London

[47] Fritz, Robert, *Corporate Tides: The Inescapable Laws of Organizational Structure*, Berrett-Koehler, San Francisco [11966]

[48] See www.RobertFritz.com

[49] Anne Lamott, *Bird by Bird: Some Instructions On Writing and Life*, Pantheon Books, New York [1994]

[50] Barbara Sher, *Wishcraft: How To Get What You Really Want*, Ballantine Books, New York [1979]

[51] Colleen Mariah Rae, *Movies in the Mind: How to Build a Short Story*, Sherman Asher Publishing, Santa Fe [1996]

[52] Kimon Nicolaides, *The Natural Way to Draw*, Houghton-Mifflin, New York [1975]

[53] Ray Bradbury, *Zen In the Art of Writing: Essays in Creativity*, Joshua Odell Editions [1994]

[54] Joyce Carol Oates, quoted in *What If? Writing Exercises for Fiction Writers*, by Anne Bernays and Pamela Painter, Harper Collins, New York [1990]

[55] Matthew Fox, *Creation Spirituality: Liberating Gifts for the Peoples of the Earth*, HarperSanFrancisco,1991]

ISBN 141200296-6

221557

Made in the USA